The
Edtech Advocate's
Guide to Leading Change in Schools

Mark Gura

International Society for Technology in Education
PORTLAND, OREGON • ARLINGTON, VIRGINIA

The Edtech Advocate's Guide to Leading Change in Schools

Mark Gura

© 2018 International Society for Technology in Education

Acquisitions Editor: *Valerie Witte*
Editor: *Emily Reed*
Copy Editor: *Barbara Hewick*
Indexer: *Wendy Allex*
Book Design and Production: *Don Gura*
Cover Design: *Edwin Ouellette*

Library of Congress Cataloging-in-Publication Data available.

First Edition
ISBN: 978-1-56484-394-4
Ebook version available.

Printed in the United States of America

ISTE® is a registered trademark of the International Society for Technology in Education.

ABOUT ISTE

The International Society for Technology in Education (ISTE) is the premier nonprofit organization serving educators and education leaders committed to empowering connected learners in a connected world. ISTE serves more than 100,000 education stakeholders throughout the world.

ISTE's innovative offerings include the ISTE Conference & Expo, one of the biggest, most comprehensive edtech events in the world—as well as the widely adopted ISTE Standards for learning, teaching and leading in the digital age and a robust suite of professional learning resources, including webinars, online courses, consulting services for schools and districts, books, and peer-reviewed journals and publications. Visit *iste.org* to learn more.

Join our community of passionate educators!

ISTE members get free year-round professional development opportunities and discounts on ISTE resources and conference registration. Membership also connects you to a network of educators who can instantly help with advice and best practices.

Join or renew your membership today! Visit *iste.org/membership* or call 800.336.5191.

ALSO BY MARK GURA

Make, Learn, Succeed: Building a Culture of Creativity in Your School

Teaching Literacy in the Digital Age: Inspiration for All Levels and Literacies

Getting Started with LEGO Robotics: A Guide for K–12 Educators

To see all books available from ISTE, please visit *iste.org/resources*.

ABOUT THE AUTHOR

 Mark Gura has been an educator for more than three decades. The former director of instructional technology for the New York City Department of Education, he began his career as a teacher and spent 18 years in elementary and middle school classrooms in Harlem. More recently, he has taught graduate education courses at Fordham University, Touro College, and New York Institute of Technology. Gura was a staff and curriculum developer for NYC's Central Division of Curriculum and Instruction before being recruited to develop and administer the first citywide instructional technology program. He has written extensively on education for the *New York Daily News*, *Converge*, and a variety of other education magazines, and has written and published numerous books on education and has spoken on the subject of instructional technology throughout the United States. He lives in Jupiter, Florida, teaching graduate teacher education courses online, as well as writing and podcasting.

Acknowledgments

The author would like to thank the following for their contributions to this book:

Jessie Boyce

Robyn McKenney

Julianne B. Ross-Kleinmann

Whitney Wadecki

Nicole Zumpano

CONTENTS

PREFACE

At every stage of creating this book, from original idea to finish, I had in mind my students: preservice and inservice K–12 teachers engaged in master's programs at two American universities. For over five years, I have taught edtech courses to graduate students in technology in education programs. These programs qualify students for certification as school technologists and educational technology specialists for placement in schools under that license category. Many of them will find their way to placement in central district offices and similar situations in which their skills will be directed at the educational technology efforts in numerous schools.

My students are deeply interested in educational technology and see taking on this specialization and expertise as a way to ensure employment in a valued field that has all the earmarks of a job type guaranteed to remain in demand. In fact, they will gain status as schools more thoroughly turn to technology as the way to get their core business done.

I firmly believe that anyone who has been paying attention to the resources and approaches that teachers, schools, and districts are currently gravitating toward is seeing a strong trend toward what I will call a "digital transition." Because of clear improvements in practicality and efficacy, virtually everything that's done in schools will be done digitally.

In the last decade, a great deal of the administrative chores of running a school—chores such as attendance, student record keeping, purchasing, payroll, and communications—have become digitized. Teaching, too, is more and more commonly accomplished with technology. Although this transformation is far along in progress, there are wide disparities in the degree to which it is happening. While nearly all districts are involved, some are ahead of the curve while a great many, for a variety of reasons, are behind. The instructional arena is where there is the most room for change and growth, and where the impact will be felt most strongly. Even in schools in which there is already an appreciable amount of instruction supported by technology, there is room for a great deal more.

The upshot is that a powerful transformational digital shift is impending. Cost efficiencies as well as improvements in efficacy guarantee that schools will become, as virtually all other work environments have, digital environments.

The question is: Are schools ready for this? In most cases the answer is: No! The issue isn't whether or not schools are ready to use or increase their use of technology. Rather, it's whether or not they are prepared to become learning and work environments in which the most common way of getting the job done, whatever job that may be, involves the use of technology.

Not only must schools, like all other organizations and institutions, be able to purchase and deploy technology; they must develop practices around its use and educate all users accordingly, as well as continuously evaluate and retarget for improvement.

This undertaking would be hard enough, yet, in addition to these critical success factors, the people who allocate funds for school technology and professional development may not fully understand it and its promise—and certainly not the impending towering wave of adoption. Further, some individuals who should be using technology, or at the very least would benefit greatly from doing so, resist learning and using it. And, of course, because many of them are good, conscientious people, we can infer that their resistance has to do with lack of understanding.

There really is little time to waste. This is a change that by all signs is bearing down upon us, soon to impact. While there may be many ways for schools, districts, and departments of education to prepare, this book takes the position that, at the very least, every school must have a staff member who is prepared to guide administrators and teachers in becoming a community of professionals who understand technology and its proper place in supporting teaching and learning, as well as those administrative and other functions that support it.

Schools will not be transformed into digital environments overnight. They will do so through a series of steps and phases that may happen at a pace unusually fast for change in education. This book is dedicated to providing some direction, information, and advice for those professionals who will take on the crucial work of guiding their schools into their logical next phase, as digital learning environments.

INTRODUCTION

The mission has changed. It wasn't long ago that educational technologists and other education professionals were focused primarily on effective ways to bring technology into schools. This is still the case, but the task has expanded, as has the vision that drives it. What we are facing now is nothing less than the complete digital transformation of our classrooms and schools.

The focus must shift from tracking myriad important items—emerging resources, evolving practices, and changes in educational approaches and goals—to one of seeing how all these items connect and fit together to form a profoundly altered, improved version of education.

Those just waking up to the enormity of the impending digital shift are dazzled and a bit dazed by what appears to be a kaleidoscope of opportunities, possibilities, and decisions. One crucial aspect is that shift this now includes everyone in the school. All who contribute to the educational experience of our students are confronted with this situation, but none more importantly than our teachers. Across the grades and curriculum areas, they are very much unprepared for the changes unfolding.

As entire school communities are impacted, it is only reasonable that they will seek out and turn to informed individuals who can guide them. The problem is that there are not nearly enough certified tech coaches in the field, and those in place are not adequately prepared to handle this new mission. While they are highly competent and capable of offering support to their colleagues in what has been up until now partial involvement with school technology, many in this position are unfamiliar with the new, more total and global version and how to support it. This is true for both those formally trained or appointed for their role as well as the many who are coming to this responsibility from other paths.

Technology-transformed education is about to be achieved, but is not yet well understood. Those who would guide and support must see, understand, and, above all, communicate effectively about this broader, more inclusive vision. How do all the pieces fit together? How does technology empower, enrich, expand, and change what teachers and students do? What is the new education that technology is leading us toward?

It is a difficult-to-juggle blend of understandings that is needed as we move into the next phase of education. One must understand technology as well as teaching and learning. This complex body of knowledge is necessary to support the change that educators have been attempting to bring about for decades, a change that, all of a sudden, is engulfing us in a powerful and rapid growth spurt.

To make the situation even more challenging, the institution of school hasn't created enough opportunities from which those who will be called on to guide the field may emerge.

Without a doubt, there are resources and programs that motivated individuals can turn to. There are books, online tools, and resources. But again, these are largely individual facets in the mosaic, many dots that somehow need to be connected.

Two Resources Worth a Look

The ISTE Essential Conditions are the 14 critical elements necessary to effectively leverage technology for learning. They offer educators and school leaders a research-backed framework to guide implementation of the ISTE Standards, tech planning, and systemwide change. Learn more at *iste.org/standards/tools-resources/essential-conditions.*

University of Florida's Technology Integration Matrix (TIM) provides a framework for describing and targeting the use of technology to enhance learning. See the TIM, videos, and more at *fcit.usf.edu/matrix*

All these resources require time to absorb, learn to use, and benefit from. And they require a "Where we are heading?" understanding that would lead one to them in the first place.

This book is intended to be a quick and handy top layer guide, while still provoking deeper thinking about the complex and highly impactful nature of educational technology. It offers a snapshot of the field that is emerging and coming into focus, observed from a 30,000-foot perspective as well as close viewing for boots on the ground implementation. In a sense, it is the confluence of seeing the big picture, explaining it to others, and helping the professional community make important decisions and take important steps to intelligently and effectively participate in this great change in education.

This book may be used by a variety of professionals looking for direction in guiding their school communities to a meaningful next step toward a comprehensive, transformative use of technology. Some may be certified technology coaches, but many will be informed colleagues from other roles, positions, and certification areas who hope to function effectively as ad hoc guides. This book is intended to serve the huge body of curriculum and instruction professionals who already lead in one capacity or another, but who now must begin to make technology a defining aspect of what they, and those they influence, do from now on.

CHAPTER 1

Digital Transformation in Education

"We imagine a school in which students and teachers excitedly and joyfully stretch themselves to their limits in pursuit of projects built on their own visions... not one that that merely succeeds in making apathetic students satisfy minimal standards."
—SEYMOUR PAPERT

The following excerpts are taken from former U.S. Secretary of Education Arne Duncan's remarks at the State Educational Technology Directors Association Education Forum. For those of us in the fields of education and educational technology, it was encouraging to learn of the Secretary's full awareness of the importance, scope, and impending impact of a full-on transformation of our schools from hard copy, brick and mortar, traditional educational institutions to digital learning environments. He opened his talk stating:

We're at an important transition point. We're getting ready to move from a predominantly print-based classroom to a digital learning environmen.... We need to leverage technology's promise to improve learning. I am optimistic because states and districts are starting to lead this transformation. (U.S. DEPARTMENT OF EDUCATION, 2010)

It was a startling speech, offering a clear description of the awesome power of technology to transform education for the better and making a strong case for the necessity to make this happen.

Unfortunately, the change he alluded to hasn't happened yet, certainly not "to scale," although, as has long been the case, there are models and pockets of schools that have achieved the state of change he described.

THAT WAS THEN. THIS IS NOW

Duncan's speech was given in 2010, and today we haven't come close to realizing the potential to transform education for the better. It's also true that this wasn't the first of this sort of speech to be made by a high-level policymaker; other speeches have been made before and since and, in that sense, we might discount this as another one of those statements intended to inspire us with uplifting visions of possible futures—futures that, if they aren't made this year, well, hopefully we'll get to them someday. After all, the need and the possibility of fulfilling this vision won't disappear, even if we carry on with business as usual for a while longer.

But, while schools may be slow to realize the potential that beckons them, the world around them has changed profoundly and continues to do so. We have arrived at a moment when deferring full commitment to this particular change is more than simply unwise.

We live in a world so dominated by technology that, for instance, stores are disappearing as online shopping replaces them; robots of all sorts are appearing in our environment, not as oddities or marvels, but as common tools and machines; and we live in a world in which machines now learn (as they were designed) to track and predict our behavior and to offer us better experiences, including learning. In short, we've run out of time. Technology has become so efficient, cost effective, and user friendly that the adoption difficulties that have allowed schools to put off becoming digital learning environments are no longer there. It simply is no longer practical, it no longer makes sense to defer allowing technology to make school a better experience for students and those who support them.

THE WORLD IS DEEPLY INVOLVED IN DIGITAL TRANSFORMATION

Consider the work environment of any of our institutions, such as medicine, banking, manufacturing, publishing, sales, and marketing. They all function on a platform composed of resources and practices defined by the technology developed to support them. These technologies are not in place as experiments or solutions to problems; they are in place because they are understood to be the very best way to get things done. This is true for virtually every field, industry, and institution we have except for one notable exception: education.

This lamentable situation has been true for over a decade. I first wrote about it in *Saving Technology for Education* (Roman and Littlefield, 2004), during a period when not only were educators resisting technologies that clearly promised to improve the field, but there was also serious pushback by naysayers who argued that technology was a negative, at best a waste of time.

This change in schools was further hampered because a great majority of inservice teachers had come of age and taken their place in the classroom before the emergence of common digital technologies for the masses. Consequently, teachers had to first learn how to handle a computer as well as specific instructional resources and understand how they could be used in teaching and learning.

Since then, much more technology has been acquired by schools and is in place, ready to be used by teachers and students. Importantly, the bodies of professional understanding, available instructional and management resources, professional development and support approaches, and so on, have been expanded and refined. The vast majority of what's needed to transform our classrooms and schools into digital age learning environments has already been developed and made available.

Still, the technology use situation in our schools can be described as partially equipped, partially adopted, and partially understood. While there is much more familiarity and acceptance than before, few have a truly comprehensive understanding, and the body of practice in implementation currently shows that to be the case. Simply stated, we are in a period of transition where much is done and much potential for more remains, although the fully crystallized version of a transformed iteration of education still belongs to the future.

WHAT'S HAPPENING AND WHY?

We are in the middle of a digital revolution in education, or perhaps a better term would be the one Secretary of Education Arne Duncan used: digital *transformation* of education. It's happening all around us and, although many educators may not see this dense forest, they are seeing a massive accumulation of trees.

A proliferation of digital learning resources—many of them free and easy to use—have become available. Numerous blogs, websites, and podcasts are dedicated to reviewing and describing how to use them. Record keeping, something that until very recently was paper-driven, is now done digitally. Schools have central digital platforms in which records are kept, annotated, and organized for reference. Administrators, teachers, students and their parents can communicate with one another in ways that enable efficient and effective transmission of information while maintaining student privacy and safety. Still, many educators see only individual resources and tools and not the wonderful interrelated ecosystem that they establish.

Teaching and learning, too, have been transformed. Locating content (books, articles, audio, and video) is much more effective with the use of technology and online sources. The web, the greatest library of human knowledge and expression ever assembled, is available to students through their internet connection. Digital content can be altered to benefit the needs of learners through the use of design, video and presentation tools. Students' response items—quizzes, essays, or media-rich presentations— are not only better produced digitally, but submitted to teachers without physical challenges and with perfect records of submissions. The isolating walls of classrooms are no longer barriers. Students can establish relationships online with peer learners around the globe and benefit from the knowledge and teaching of experts and teacher specialists outside their school. Many elements of the experience of learning have now been vastly improved and expanded by technology.

WHAT THIS MEANS FOR SCHOOLS

This new education environment is inspiring. It fosters exhilaration about school and education, something that hasn't been seen in many places for a long time. However, in order to bring it into widespread implementation, much has to be done and many decisions have to be made.

While there are many resources with which to establish a digital platform that an entire school (or district) can jointly use to take care of its administrative and managerial functions, once a decision is made on which resource to acquire, the community will develop over time a culture and body of practice to use it.

In the realm of teaching and learning, there is much depth, complexity, and, likely, transformation of goals, methods, and culture. This is so because technology offers the possibility of not just doing things better, but of doing better things, a crucial distinction for technology change agents to grasp and explain to colleagues.

Transformation is not an exaggeration here. Technology allows for students, as they always have, to read (or otherwise gather knowledge from) content items. However, even at this simple level, it is possible for each student to find or be presented with (by the teacher) a content item that is far better suited to his or her individual needs as a learner, which is a transformative change.

Beyond this simple, classic approach to teaching and learning—the distribution of content, reflection and discussion, and proof that one has learned it through quizzes or essays—technology enables other, new types of activities that were previously beyond the reach of teachers and students. These include approaches like project based learning, personalized learning, distance collaboration, and hybrid learning.

An important early "ah ha" in a community's transition to a digital environment involves tackling the question, "Should schools be teaching *about* technology, or teaching and fostering learning *with* technology, or should they be doing both?" Importantly, educators currently are not simply teaching technology as another subject, that is, as a body of discreet skills and information. Rather, they are approaching technology education as part and parcel of the body of new ways that humans engage with information and the world.

This point was discussed in an interview in *Education Week* magazine with former teacher and edtech expert, Will Richardson. According to Richardson, "Schools need to revolutionize teaching and learning to keep pace with societal changes" (REBORA, 2010).

He went on to say:

> *I feel like the change [in schools] has been glacial.... [I]t's a huge culture shift. Education by and large has been a very closed type of profession. "Just let me close my doors and teach"—you hear that refrain all the time." [T]his change must involve all members of the school community* (REBORA, 2010).

Richardson described the transformation of education and what must change. Here are some of the takeaways from the interview:

Teachers must have an online presence. Doing so can model the importance of effective digital portfolios, participation, and positive online footprints for students who will be "searched for on the web— over and over again."

Without sharing, there is no education. Educators should be willing to share and collaborate while making new connections and working in networks that can really enhance learning.

Network literacy is a key 21st century skill. Students should be encouraged to create their own communities and networks, engage with others around the world and navigate learning opportunities beyond the school walls.

Emphasize learning over knowledge. Instead of looking for the right answer, teaching and assessments should focus on the learning process and how students use creativity and critical thinking to solve problems.

Some things can't be learned in a workshop. Professional development must change to a learning culture where educators are immersed in digital technologies and allowed to practice. (REBORA, 2010).

THE JOURNEY AHEAD

The road ahead for the field of education, unavoidably, will involve heavy focus on the shift from a traditional, paper-driven, face-to-face platform that supports and stages teaching and learning to one that is based on digital technologies. The practical advantages of digital resources and the way they enable the implementation of long-sought-after practices makes this shift something that will continue to assume greater and greater importance.

As an example, we can think of the approach of personalized learning. Moving beyond the "one size fits all" reality of teaching from a single textbook, assumed to be adequate for all students in a class or school, is truly only possible with the use of technology. The amount of effort required to search out personalized content items that would better suit each and every student's learning needs and interests, in concert with the demands of distance and access involved in visiting an endless array of libraries required to do so, precludes this from being done, even though educational theorists have been desirous of realizing this ideal for many decades.

And while not all educational policymakers and administrators may prioritize bringing this vision to full realization, there are other implementation factors to be considered. Access to open educational resource (OER) digital content items that make for a personalized experience also allows for a great deal of free content to be acquired. It can be made available without need for storage, archiving, and focused retrieval—all costly and demanding aspects of implementation—or for the continual updating of material in view of relevance and efficacy as instructional materials. These practicalities, particularly when understood as being present in addition to highly improved pedagogical value, ensure that digital resource-based instruction will demand the attention of educators.

The above example is but one of a very large body of impressive improvements and advantages to be had by the shift to a digital platform for education. However, it should be noted that, while the serious investigation and consideration of this sort of change can be convincing and inspiring, the institution of school continues to run in largely traditional mode in many places and ways; so much so that the weight of the traditional, even when viewed through the lens of its dubious efficacy, can easily obscure a vision of how things may be improved by a shift to a digital platform.

Consequently, expending some time and effort to see the new landscape and functioning of educational institutions that digital platforms will support and precipitate is an important aspect of participating in manifesting it as well as in using it. The section that follows offers an understanding of this new learning environment, a vision for how to establish it, and the requisite facets of working and learning there.

CHAPTER 2

The New Classroom

"If you don't know where you are going, any road will get you there." —LEWIS CARROLL

When thinking about the digital transformation of education, it's easy to conjure up visions of a futuristic, Jetson-like school with robot teachers, levitating classrooms, students learning while asleep, and so on. We are fascinated with such fanciful visions for good reason. For while the classroom that is described in novels set in the 19th century is one that no longer truly serves our population, it still, in many ways, continues to define the contemporary school experience.

Such classrooms, no doubt, will give way to newer learning environments, but what will the new classroom be like? Will it be defined by an accumulation of new technology items, or a body of changes to support technology use that stem from innovations in architecture and interior design? Will it be a set of promising new teaching and learning practices and, perhaps, a new classroom culture to support them?

It's important for the digital change agent to develop a good sense of what we might call the digital learning environment. In other words, what is perceived as the ideal situation for teaching and learning that will result from the development and adoption of practice that embraces technology, and how technology will function to appropriately and effectively support the brand of teaching and learning that is truly needed and is evolving.

This chapter will explore the many elements of the digital learning environment, including the physical setting, the digital infrastructure, and the body of devices that reside there; from the instructional resources and practices to apply them, to the body of understandings and goals that validate and guide the use of technology in the context of education.

FROM TRADITIONAL CLASSROOM TO DIGITAL LEARNING ENVIRONMENT

If one were to search the web for a term like "digital learning environment of the future," one would come across descriptions of ideal alternatives to the current, traditional classroom. These would include descriptions of everything from floor to ceiling digital displays, wired and Wi-Fi-enabled soundproof study spaces, and student personal devices. It's worth noting that often such visions of "the school of tomorrow" are offered by technology vendors and the entertainment industry.

In all likelihood, though, a very opposite reality is the one that school digital change agents will face for some time to come. The institution of school changes very slowly. While even those schools built recently *may* have a modern look and feel, and may have some elegant and creative use of common and specialized spaces, deeply ingrained functional aspects of school still feature traditional reliance on separated classrooms that are set for 30 students, more or less, with simple, moveable desks and chairs. The key point here is that these instructional spaces were not designed for technology use. They are generic, intended to be useful for whatever instructional activity is to go on in them and with the understanding that teachers will make slight modifications (like the layout of the moveable furniture) to make them suitable for the grade and subject being taught. In many, the original electrical wiring, lighting, and other physical attributes are set features, although certainly many classrooms have had their wiring modified somewhat to accommodate increased need. Of course, modifications of all sorts can be made, but these require dealing with bureaucratic, political, budgetary, and other negotiations that likely are beyond the capacity to navigate by educators who are focused, appropriately, on improving teaching and learning.

In view of the above, in understanding classroom tech use, and especially in planning for it, it's wise to survey and understand the capacity and suitability of classrooms in which the technology will be employed—and to do so from the point of view of technology use—ahead of making decisions. Education has a long history of inspired and well-intentioned colleagues making plans and purchases based on the potential of resources, without considering the specific environment in which they will be used, only to find out down the road that implementation was less than desired because of the features of the classroom itself.

OUTREACH AND PARTNERSHIPS

It is unlikely that those who take on the work of digital change agent will have deep experience and expertise in selecting and maintaining hardware, nor is it likely that those who have this essential knowledge set will take on that work. One approach is to partner with those who do, either within the district or by reaching out to those whom the district outsources solutions to this need. Perhaps even better and easier would be to join a professional learning network (PLN) for school technologists. There may be such a PLN or discussion board already set up in your district. Another option is the ISTE Technology Coordinators' Network, an active group of a few thousand good folks who have, in the aggregate, accrued an awesome body of this type of knowledge and who generously share information and opinion in this area.

RESOURCES THAT SUPPORT LEARNING IN THE DIGITAL AGE

Currently, there is much activity in the acquisition, adoption, and implementation of digital technology in our schools and classrooms. Unfortunately, a good deal of this can be characterized as schools simply "doing technology"—in other words, conforming to a current trend and fad in the field without truly understanding the full implications and far-reaching meaning of doing so. Many are chasing short-term advantages and improvements piecemeal, without awareness of how the various pieces fit together and the picture they will form when eventually all are in place.

With the constant emergence of digital resources (many of them free or "open") and requirements to adopt them from districts or state departments of education or from funders or other interested parties that are focused on single, specific uses of technology, it is small wonder that school communities are encouraged to embrace individual items to perform individual functions, without much regard to how they all may fit sensibly into an ever-increasing body of digital additions to the world teachers work in.

Consequently, there's much involvement in "doing" without benefit of a big picture awareness of what it all means. To help make sense from this growing, potentially confusing mass, every school needs members of its community who see and can share a big picture understanding. Without that, much may be done, but arrival at a worthwhile destination is doubtful.

The other major dimension to the new, digital learning environment is composed of the resources that run on devices and that directly shape the activities in which students are engaged. In supporting the school community to embrace this new learning environment, the learning management system (or LMS) is a valuable, supportive resource.

What's an LMS and Why Opt to Use One?

In short, an LMS is a common virtual platform designed to make it easy for teachers and students to access resources from multiple sources. It's a home base, a platform that members of the school community can use to participate in the online life of the school and their class. It can function as an extended group or public communications resource, and can support the work and activities of learners as individuals or in small groups. It can be a vehicle for teachers to share information with students in their classes, to distribute assignments, and to receive completed work; they can provide feedback and grades, and keep records of all things that happen in the LMS environment. Beyond all this, using the LMS becomes an enlightening immersion in classroom technology for newcomers to this dimension of education, one that supports users as they become comfortable technology and explore its dimensions.

In her article titled "LMS Enhances K12 Instruction," Katie Kilfoyle Remis, states:

> *Without an LMS, teachers and students trying to access online education tools must sign in and out of multiple applications, including open education resources, subscription-based learning programs, and websites that teachers created for their courses. Teachers also need to log in to the student information system and administrative applications, such as grade books.* (REMIS, 2015)

If your school hasn't adopted an LMS yet, or is contemplating doing so, this is one "square one starting point" to take seriously. It is a low-cost (no cost in many respects), simple, and effective way for a school to begin transformatively integrating technology. Further, schools that begin this way soon have deep experience with a model that can later account for other types of technology integration.

In conducting one of my online graduate-level courses for practicing teachers who intend to become school technologists, one of my students volunteered that he felt that the approach taken by his school (inner-city New York City) was a wise one. His school had adopted a small handful of technology items that were used across the grades, classes, and subjects. These included class sets of laptops (one rolling cart in which the laptops are secured and charged), interactive whiteboards in most classrooms, and an LMS for all classes. This approach allows schools that are just emerging from minimal technology use to have a vibrant tech use program, but one that is simple enough to ensure success as the school grows into deeper tech use, building on successes without being overwhelming. By deploying just a small handful of devices, albeit devices that are highly flexible and can accommodate many varieties of digital content, learning activities, and approaches to instruction, the school (or at least a good portion of it) can move as a whole into new stages of the evolution of education. There are fewer key skills for which teachers need professional development, fewer types of technical issues to address when things go wrong, and a more uniform way for the school culture to change as it embraces the new.

Google Classroom

As is the case for the school mentioned above, the LMS (whether a full blown, true LMS or a similar resource tapped to function as one) can prove to be an important initial resource for schools attempting to expand their technology use program to a fully comprehensive one. There are numerous choices for this category of resource. Many schools have opted to adopt Google Classroom, a free and easy to use resource, as their LMS. In a review on the Common Sense Education blog, teacher Marjorie P. describes Google Classroom as follows:

> Simply put, Google Classroom serves as the mission control for your classroom— incorporating communication, collaboration, and assessment in one shared, digital space. Teachers create virtual classrooms for each of their classes. Students then join the classroom using a class code. The stream section functions a lot like a Facebook wall where teachers can post assignments, questions, announcements, and so on. Students are also able to post announcements, including multimedia posts. Parents receive daily or weekly summaries of student work and announcements. Parents and guardians can remain totally in the loop and correspond with teachers. The possibilities with Google Classroom are endless because it integrates with the GAFE apps and with other teaching tools as well. (COMMON SENSE MEDIA, 2017)

DEVICES AND INFRASTRUCTURE

The above sections focus on how technology interfaces with practice and curricular needs and the ways the school is organized to address them. This is in keeping with well-thought-out priorities. Unfortunately, in the history of evolving digital learning environments, educators have mistakenly made devices and infrastructure the top priority. This leaves them in the position of figuring out what they can do, from the instructional point of view, with the technology they have already invested in, rather than first informing themselves about what's possible in terms of technology-redefined teaching and learning, then deciding on which approaches and practices they want to make part of their program, and only then acquiring the devices and infrastructure necessary to do so.

Three Teaching Modalities and How Technology Can Support Them

One important way to understand and plan for devices and infrastructure is to focus on the ways that teachers work with students. While there are many, an easy way to look at this is that teachers are generally assigned to work with classes of roughly 30 students. In order to maximize instructional impact, teachers will teach in three modalities:

1. They'll conduct whole-class lessons and discussions.

2. They'll direct students (most frequently when they are seated in a whole-class configuration) to work independently (this includes doing homework and independent research and projects).

3. They'll create (or direct students to form their own) small study or work groups, generally of two to four students each. This is a long-proven practice.

To see if your planning is on track, ask "Does the technology available to teachers and students support all three modalities?"

The whole-class modality has been neatly handled by the use of interactive whiteboards. These function as a large-screen display that all class members can see during whole-class lessons and discussions. Some teachers also encourage students in small groups or individually to use these, when appropriate, to support learning.

Some schools have successfully taken the approach of standardizing technology use with the distribution and deployment of just a few varieties of common classroom devices, such as interactive whiteboards, digital document cameras, and mobile carts with classroom sets of laptops or tablets. They train the teachers in their use (both how to operate them physically, handle them from the classroom management perspective, and how to use them in teaching). By limiting the universe of what they use (at least in the early stages of digitally transforming themselves), schools simplify and manage what might be seen as an overwhelming body of work and change.

Class sets of laptops, Chromebooks, or tablets (e.g., iPads) are easy to use to support paired or small-group instruction, with groups or pairs often sharing the device. This may be done to extend the usefulness of such devices when there isn't a single device available for every student or because there is some instructional advantage in doing so.

Ideally, there is a single device available for each student for those times that the teacher, acting as instructional designer, feels that individual work best supports the learning that is targeted. Other times the sharing takes place in order to give a degree of access to each student, although the impact of sharing may be that it detracts as sharing a book might.

School Technology for Administrative Tasks

While the major thrust of a school's full realization of the potential of technology to enable it to provide the best experience possible for students should be the way technology impacts teaching and learning, we should note briefly that, toward that end, there are numerous administrative chores schools must handle. Importantly, these relate to student learning, too, in the sense that when technology is applied, it can free up all parties to devote more time and energy to the school's core business, teaching and learning. These chores are unavoidable and can get in the way of teaching and learning. They include attendance, student records, communicating with parents and collecting paperwork from them, communications throughout the staff, and administrative needs (like buses, lunch, fees, extracurricular activities, etc.) that more often are better handled through the wide variety of emerging digital resources.

FEATURES OF THE DIGITAL LEARNING ENVIRONMENT

Digital devices, infrastructure, and bandwidth are not what constitute the digital learning environment. They should be considered as resources required to establish and support the environment. Although it would be pointless, one could use connected devices and the digital resources that run on them simply to transcribe teaching and learning as it has existed for a very long time into a digital version that would barely scratch the surface of what technology can help accomplish. Some of the most salient features of this new environment are briefly identified and explained below.

Learning ABOUT Technology vs. Learning WITH Technology

For many, the hardest part of the digital shift to understand is that the primary place and purpose of technology in our schools is not to have students learn about technology itself.

Yes, we want them to know the basics of technology, to gain some understanding of how it works and pick up some of its key skills, like simple programming and coding, just as we want them to understand and know a bit about everything important that goes on in and shapes the world. However, by far the greatest point of technology use programs is the way that the technology transforms how people think and work and communicate. It does this profoundly in the real world beyond school— those are the things that technology was created to do in the first place—and we want to bring the power of that transformation into the nature and quality of the educational experience we offer our students.

21st Century Skills

One group that has studied technology's impact and resultant changes in thought, work, and communication is the Partnership for 21st Century Skills (P21), which has produced a good deal of material to explain it—much of it with significant implications for the field of education. Examining the body of work P21 has generated, one sees that it has identified areas of learning that are either new to the digital age or that have assumed a particularly high importance in it. These are all associated with technology, but are not technology in and of themselves.

At the core of the group's work is the P21 Framework, which represents 21st century student outcomes, organized into four areas:

- **KEY SUBJECTS:** English and world language arts, arts, STEM subjects, and social studies

- **LEARNING AND INNOVATION:** critical thinking, communication, collaboration, and creativity, often referred to as the four Cs

- **LIFE AND CAREER SKILLS AND INFORMATION:** flexibility and adaptability, initiative and self-direction, social and cross-cultural skills, productivity and accountability, leadership and responsibility

- **MEDIA, AND TECHNOLOGY SKILLS:** creating, evaluating, and effectively using information, media, and technology

Note that while the framework represents these areas distinctly for descriptive purposes, P21 views all the components as fully interconnected in the process of 21st century teaching and learning. Moreover, the framework lists the support systems of standards and assessments, curriculum and instruction, professional development, and learning environments as essential elements.

Digital Content

The most traditional and classic approach to education involves distributing content to students; having them review and reflect on it; discussing the content that's been consumed in whole-class discussions or through one-on-one questions; having students respond to it in quiz, test, essay, or other format to check on what's been learned; and then either addressing gaps in what's been learned or moving on to the next theme.

Education reformers have long found problems with this approach. One is that the content itself is too limited to produce good learning results for our very inclusive school populations. The new digital content, however, has the potential to afford great flexibility in a number of ways.

Format

A great deal of teaching and learning has traditionally been accommodated by the use of the classic textbook, which set identical material before each student. Add a few collections of essays or short stories and class subscriptions to periodicals and that pretty much sums up the material that drove (in many cases, still drives) school over the past 150 years. Digital content allows for the format (the size, style, font, color, and so on) to be varied, may provide some portions in media (such as animations, video, and sound clips), and may be searched for specific items. Some versions allow for teachers to customize the content for specific classes and students, by annotating content and adding links to related content. Teachers may even be able to track which items have been consumed and responded to by students. The possibilities for customizing the content are vast, and producers often upgrade by incorporating features and tools from recently emerged resources, such as new channels for sharing via social media applications.

Distribution

With digital content, it's possible for a class to receive a variety of texts, perhaps with different individuals receiving different versions or titles. In addition to the burden of carrying books back and forth from home to school, shortages often necessitated sharing books, which, in turn, required schools to allow students access to texts only when in class or at specific, narrow bands of time. With digital distribution of content, students may access content from a device when and where they need it, obviating carrying copies and allowing them access when school is not in session.

Expense

Providers now often include supplemental items and services to make purchase of their materials more attractive. Digital content has spawned a significant body of free or *open* content.

Interactivity

Digital content is flexible and interactive. Students will find hyperlinks in the text, enabling them to explore subject connections that seem interesting or appealing, to view embedded when interested, and to use embedded tools (like audio text readers or reading pacers) to support and customize their experience of consuming content.

Simulations / Visualizing Content and Concepts

Traditional textbooks called for students to learn about things by reading descriptions and perhaps by seeing some photos or illustrations. There are many subjects that students need to see unfold in order for them to visualize and understand the material. The germination of a seed is one example; the splitting of an atom is another. Other topics, like the eruption of a volcano, are far too dangerous to be done in actuality, yet are difficult to comprehend from mere narrative description. Such topics can be understood through the use of digital media.

Blended Learning

In essence, the blend refers to online learning mixed with face-to-face learning. The online portion may be accessed by the students in school, often under the supervision of a teacher. In a flipped classroom, the student may access the online portion of the program at home or elsewhere, with class time set aside for face-to-face exchanges with teachers and fellow students.

The blended approach has several advantages. First, some students benefit from the independence from school. Some may have social difficulties or logistical issues in physically getting to a brick-and-mortar school. Students may be permitted to learn through a much higher degree of control over the time, place, path, or pace of learning. Second, a school may have a teaching staff limited in its abilities (for example, in foreign languages) and may extend its range of learning opportunities by offering courses monitored in the local school but hosted and originated elsewhere.

Data-Driven Instruction and Adaptive Learning

Most educators lament the poor quantity and quality of information to be had when trying to assess if material has been learned or not. A quiz gives little information about what hasn't been learned and why, nor does the very slow flow of the data it provides do much to inform the ongoing instruction.

Technology can track the content consumption, response habits, learning quality, and accuracy of students who interact with it. Technology can reconfigure the content and response requests on an ongoing basis as the learner interacts with it. One example of this is the adaptive courseware provider Knewton, which was described in a post on the EdSurge blog.

> *"After the teacher assigns a lesson, the system will give students pretests to assess their knowledge, and then deliver different sequences of learning materials and assessments based on how they progress. Teachers can also upload their own materials, which will be tagged with metadata about their subject, standards, and other information that can be used by Knewton's adaptive learning algorithms."* (EDSURGE, 2015)

We have arrived at the beginning of this sort of digital learning resource and the road ahead is a fascinating and likely very rich one.

Connected Learning

One of the most transformative aspects of technology for education is the expansion of the platform for teaching and learning achieved by having classrooms online and connected to the internet. Before the digital era, teachers had access to an extremely limited selection of content materials. The internet now provides access to the greatest collection of content items ever assembled, as well as a vast number of possible peer learners, mentors, teachers, experts, and others who may impact and broaden the educational experience.

Being connected establishes a condition in which some long-valued approaches to teaching and learning may finally be implemented. For example, providing students with a personalized learning experience has been an unrealized goal for a long time; with access to the vast body of content online, it becomes possible to locate items of interest for each student. Better yet, they can search to find items of interest to themselves.

Tech-Supported Collaborative Learning

Another dimension of the transformed learning experience is to be had through the use of social media resources such as Facebook and the social learning group work facets of Edmodo, Schoology, and other increasingly popular online resources. The longstanding practice of organizing students into groups to learn collaboratively is easier to facilitate with technology, rather than attempting to do so solely in the face-to-face version of the classroom.

CHANGING TO A DIGITAL PLATFORM FOR TEACHING AND LEARNING

All things change, including the goals of education and the form it takes to realize its goals. These are currently undergoing deep changes due to the emergence and adoption of digital technology.

There are actually two strong dynamics at work. First, the ways that schools get their work done—including their physical characteristics, the resources they use, and the ways they organize students for participation—are all changing to take advantage of and to accommodate digital technologies.

Second, the bodies of concept and practice that define teaching and learning are also changing, for a variety of technology-driven reasons. Better practices and understandings of why they are advantageous have emerged and are now practical to implement due to the power and availability of technology.

For example, project based learning (PBL), an approach and practice that has attracted interest from progressive educators for a long time, has become more appealing and popular than ever because of the ways that digital technologies make it practical for all to embrace. One aspect of PBL requires students to do significant amounts of research, both on what work has been done on their chosen theme before they begin their work as well as to gather information from a wide variety of sources to use in the creation of their project. Before students had easy access to the web, such research would have been so prohibitively difficult and slow that such projects would have been too impractical for teachers to offer students as learning activities. The creation of student products, the central focus of the practice of PBL, would also have been too difficult for most to take on. Currently, though, with easy to use and near ubiquitous digital resources like desktop publishing programs, audio and video creation tools, and resources that easily generate graphics, creating student products that have the function and feel of professional work is within the grasp of most students—a powerful and impactful change established by a host of technology resources commonly used in our schools.

 ACTIVITY

HOW DOES TECHNOLOGY IMPROVE TEACHING AND LEARNING?

How does technology make it possible for the teacher to be more effective? How does technology make learning possible in situations where it wasn't possible or less likely before its implementation? How does technology enable the expansion of the curriculum, the variety of activities a school can provide students? How does technology enable better understanding of students' abilities to learn, what they have learned, and how to use that information to foster better, more effective learning?

In a table, list seven to ten examples of transformative technology use in teaching and learning, ways that technology makes them significantly better. Describe practices and resources to support them and write brief before-and-after descriptions of the application of technology to specific activities and goals listed.

Nine Ways Technology Can Transform Teaching and Learning

The following section offers glimpses into some of the most common and meaningful ways that technology transforms the essential activities that are comprised in teaching and learning, the ways that students participate, and some approaches and philosophies that establish and legitimize the context for them.

This may be used as a reference for envisioning the ways that specific schools can align themselves with how schools are using technology to evolve into digital age learning environments. It may also serve as a touchstone to determine how much change a school will plan to take on and why. The elements of transforming the learning environment include:

FROM PRINT CONTENT TO DIGITAL: Traditionally, students and teachers have used print textbooks, class sets of which have each student using an identical copy created with the average student in mind. Digital content allows for each student to have a version that can be personalized and to access it wherever and whenever needed.

FROM HARD COPY STUDENT RESPONSE TO DIGITAL: Moving to a digital platform allows students to respond to teacher challenges and prompts employing many means of representation, many of which are just right for learner needs. Likewise, teachers can respond to students using a wide range of media and can archive and retrieve student work much more efficiently.

FROM HARD COPY TEACHER GRADE BOOKS AND PHYSICAL DESK TO LMS: The now common learning management system (LMS) is a networked, master platform that allows teachers to efficiently distribute content and assignments as well as track student attendance, calculate performance, and adjust instruction based on the information gathered.

REAL-WORLD LEARNING: Technology makes practical a long-sought dimension of grounding student activities in real-world contexts.

(continued on next page)

PROJECT-BASED LEARNING (PBL): PBL has been around for a very long time. However, the logistical and practical aspects of it can be challenging for teachers who have limited time and resources. With technology, projects are facilitated and made student-friendly, allowing students the satisfaction of creating professional-looking products.

DATA-DRIVEN INSTRUCTION: Teachers have always kept data on student performance. However, collecting the data and using it in a timely manner has been difficult. Digital content can collect and analyze data about student learning on an ongoing basis, making assessment practical and allowing for better instruction.

ADAPTIVE LEARNING AND ADAPTIVE ASSESSMENT: Technology can be applied to learn about the student's learning abilities, preferences, needs, and styles. Based on this information, the student receives material that is tailored to his or her needs and that establishes a unique, personal learning experience.

GROUP AND SOCIAL LEARNING: Theories like constructivist learning make a strong case for learning socially. However, it is a commonly held belief among teachers that social learning presents problems, especially in classroom management: breaking classes up into smaller work groups strains their ability to monitor students. With the emergence of social networking resources like Edmodo, students participate in virtual work groups, and the teacher, with the support of the digital platform, can track their activity and communicate with them directly in the system to give feedback and suggestions.

EXPANDED PLATFORM FOR STUDENT ENGAGEMENT: Classes connected to the web may transcend the physical limitations of space and distance and time. Students can be connected to individuals who represent important learning resources like the authors of books the class is reading, politicians, scientists (NASA is one source), and others. They can engage in collaboration and co-learning experiences with classes of students in other countries, giving each class the experience of practicing the other's native language. Students can work in virtual labs and access online library materials, regardless of the day of the week or time of day.

A school's technology leader, especially in the role of digital change agent, will need to be informed about and balance several sets of goals for the use of technology:

TECHNOLOGY-SPECIFIC LEARNING: Proper and effective use of devices and digital resources needed for teaching and learning across the curriculum, as well as specific technology skills as goals unto themselves, like coding, programming, web design, and robotics.

LEARNING MADE POSSIBLE OR BETTER ACROSS THE CURRICULUM: Visualization resources like virtual dissection in biology courses, online research skills for history courses, classroom to writer's studio Skype sessions for ELA, and so on.

LOCALLY REQUIRED LEARNING: Local (school or district) adolescent health or safety awareness sessions, school-to-work local industry preparation learning, or local student projects-based learning efforts.

In numerous ways, digital change agents will need to understand the nature and extent of the role technology plays in each of these bodies of approaches to teaching and learning. Further, they will either need to be able to explain these approaches themselves or arrange for others to do so. The extent to which the school engages with technology and the impact it will have on the school's instructional culture and curriculum development will be greatly impacted by how convincing and inspiring these explanations are.

REMOVING BARRIERS TO MEANINGFUL TECHNOLOGY INTEGRATION

Knowing and understanding the emerging landscape of teaching and learning—what's out there and how it differs from the place where we have been teaching and learning for well over a century—is a crucial initial step for the digital change agent. In essence, there is a broad new dimension to education. No community of educators can occupy all of it, nor would they want to. However, before the particular niche that best nourishes each community can be found (or created), the full territory should be known.

One of the great impediments to much broader adoption, more meaningful integration, and reaping the abundance of benefits from instructional technology has been the misperception that technology is not truly part and parcel of the body of overarching goals and practices of mainstream education. It has been viewed as something separate and apart, a discrete set of skills and understandings that are different from the mainstream. At times this notion of technology has been respected, even sought by administrators and policymakers, who see technology as a body of skills and activities associated with successful employment after graduation. In that sense, either reluctantly or enthusiastically, it's been acknowledged as necessary student preparation for the real world.

This notion is better than the alternative: ignoring or marginalizing technology as a niche body of knowledge. Still, this lack of comprehension of, and appreciation for, the greatest potentials of technology by instructional supervisors and school administrators often leads them to see little true value and purpose in making technology a part of what goes on in classrooms across the curriculum. As a result, they often establish token examples of technology adoption and integration in the school and view this as entirely sufficient.

Small wonder, then, that for so many years and in so many schools the technology program was defined by a computer lab or two, divorced from the mainstream of the school's instructional efforts. In such labs, "computer teachers" taught students *about* technology, teaching everything from the design of computers, to keyboarding, to file management, to simple web design, to coding and programming (which has experienced a recent spurt of high interest.) What has been missing, however, is the crucial understanding that technology is in direct and strong alignment with the most sought-after and often elusive goals in education. Further, it actually is a highly effective way to make such approaches and practices implementable. In fact, one would be on firm ground observing that, for a number of practices, technology represents the only way to bring them to life.

Ironically, some of the high-profile considerations that do drive what receives a good deal of effort and attention in our schools, such as standardized testing, don't relate well to technology as facilitator or enabler. Such tests are increasingly being digitized as a way to implement and grade them more practically, but their format, most often, encompasses short responses and thinking skills that are low on Bloom's Taxonomy. Yet instructional technology has the ability to make possible and practical the teaching and learning of more complex and higher-order skills, a true step forward for instruction.

And yes, there are many digital resources either designed for, or adapted and dedicated to, preparing students for success on standardized tests, even though that preparation is not directed at teaching the types of improved learning that the era of tech is ushering in. While this may earn technology some short-term respect, it does not promote technology's association with its greatest potential to improve education by supporting and facilitating unique, individual, and spontaneous responses to experience and solutions to real-world problems.

By seeing the obvious and logical relationship between technology and important and highly sought-after instructional goals, a crucial barrier to the adoption of technology can be surmounted.

CHAPTER 3

Digital Transformation Tools and Frameworks

"You can't expect to meet the challenges of today with yesterday's tools and expect to be in business tomorrow."
—ANONYMOUS

As the old saying goes, "A journey of a thousand miles begins with a single step." So too with any digital transformation effort, hopefully with a first step that is well-thought-out and done on firm footing. And while we are making good use of travel metaphors, let's also be mindful that no matter how good our first steps may feel, they need to point us in the right direction toward a carefully chosen destination.

The section that follows features the fruits of the planning and implementation of digital transformation efforts of many. Here we see representations of the experiences of traveling the road that have been distilled into frameworks that others who are about to set out on their own journeys may use to guide them.

In the aggregate, these frameworks comprise a body of process tools. The principal takeaways here go far beyond the literal use of any of these items "as is." On the contrary, they best serve as models of how the process can be understood and planned for, especially by adapting their ideas for use at the local level or as a source of inspiration and insight into the journey ahead.

MICROSOFT'S EDUCATION TRANSFORMATION FRAMEWORK

Microsoft released a whitepaper in 2015 titled "Education Transformation Framework: Best-Practice Guidance for Successful School System Change," which can serve as a model for thinking holistically about the process of transforming schools to digital learning environments. The PDF version can be downloaded from *http://bit.ly/2j2AAC4*.

According to the authors, "School systems are faced with both a challenge and an extraordinary opportunity. The chance to rethink and reinvent education to support our most valuable asset: youth" (MICROSOFT CORPORATION, 2015).

They then pose three essential questions regarding change in education:

- Why do some countries succeed?

- How can we learn from their experience?

- How can you adapt approaches from successful education systems?

Importantly, this segment reinforces the power and necessity of starting with a vision for a comprehensive technology use program in the school and amplifies the understanding that, ultimately, this process is an important opportunity to rethink and reestablish what teachers do in their classrooms as more up to date and relevant. A great many of my students, even though they are on a learning and career track to serve schools and districts as instructional technology leaders, fail to see the relevance of this vital step. But this phase truly is a rich opportunity.

At the heart of the document is the segment titled "Ten Critical Components of School Transformation." The components are organized into two categories: leadership and policy, and 21st century pedagogy.

LEADERSHIP AND POLICY

1. Establishing a vision

2. Partnerships and capacity building for change

3. Organizational capacity, strategic planning, and quality assurance

4. Inclusion, accessibility, and sustainability

21ST CENTURY PEDAGOGY

5. Personalized learning

6. Teacher and leader capacity

7. Curriculum and assessment

8. Developing a learning community

9. Physical learning environments

10. Designing technology for effective and efficient schools (MICROSOFT CORPORATION, 2015)

The document gives more definition and insight into each of these components; at the very least, this list offers insight into the implementation and success factors that should be considered when establishing plans for an ongoing initiative to expand a school community's technology use program to a fully comprehensive one. A simple but powerful exercise would be simply to account for how each of the ten factors listed is addressed in the school community's own planning.

While this document, in a variety of ways, presents important ideas from the perspective of entire school systems, the majority of ideas have high relevance for people working to effect important change on a local level as well.

Clearly some of these ideas will resonate more for people working on the level of the individual school. Still, with a little imagination, and through some collaborative discussions with others involved in the work in the same school or in similar work in neighbor or sister schools, the importance and relevance of the framework will reveal itself. It is probably wise to see each component as something that will have to be embraced at some point during the overall process, while still seeing some as more immediately accessible than others.

EDUCATION TRANSFORMATION TECHNOLOGY ADOPTION BLUEPRINT

Another approach to representing the transformation of the learning environment from one with little or episodic use of technology to one in which the use of technology is central to the school's mission is Intel's Education Transformation Technology Adoption Blueprint, which can be viewed at *http://bit.ly/2j2sAkN*.

In this table, Intel plots stages of technology adoption, with ratios of students to computers, from one end of the spectrum to the other. This model sees adoption of technology to support teaching and learning as being marked by the ratio of available digital devices to students. The table offers further insights by showing what sorts of transformed learning activities students will typically be able to engage in at the various stages of adoption. Similarly, it includes required actions to bring this transformation about, steps like planning, budgeting, and curriculum development. The continuum notably describes success, with the early stages marked by students having "basic knowledge of technology" and the final depicted stage marked as students having mastered "21st Century Skills that prepare them to be competitive in the workforce" (INTEL CORPORATION, N.D.).

USING THE SAMR MODEL TO GUIDE DIGITAL TRANSFORMATION

Focusing on the ways teachers and students actually use technology in the processes of teaching and learning, we come to the SAMR model—SAMR stands for Substitution, Augmentation, Modification, Redefinition—a model that draws comparisons between learning that is supported by the traditional, paper-driven, hard copy environment and learning that is realized on a digital platform.

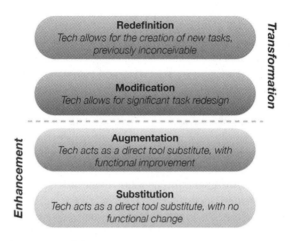

Figure 3.1. The SAMR Model

This model is particularly revealing as it divides the four levels and stages of technology use into two categories—using technology to enhance and using technology to transform—a distinction that gets to the very heart of the shift to a digital platform for teaching and learning.

This brings me to an anecdote about an experience I had some 20 years ago. I was the director of instructional technology for the New York City school system at the time and was invited to accompany one of the members of the board of education to a school in the far reaches of upper Manhattan. This school was considered something of a model of technology use because a teacher there had students using laptops in their classwork, something that at the time was considered cutting edge. Yes, educators at the time were moved by the inspiring possibility of technology for education, but were hard-pressed to figure out how to use it.

Alas, the lesson I saw was one in which bad teaching was translated from bad teaching in a hard-copy environment to bad teaching in a digital environment. This teacher had her very well-behaved and obviously bright students copying passages from a print textbook into their laptop, using a word processing program. Yes, it was most impressive to see sixth graders handling their laptops well, keyboarding and managing files, but what was the purpose of the lesson? Transcribing text from print to digital didn't enhance learning.

Now we have an approach that is more analytical and demands that clear advantages be seen in using technology before we can point to its use as something noteworthy, improving, or transformative. Thus, plotting the work of the students I observed that day, clearly what they were doing was simply substituting digital for print. However, once they had succeeded in transcribing their page of text, they might have greatly enhanced its value by using the word processor to experiment and redesign the text they had transcribed, selecting a font type, size, style, and color, and on and on, until something more appealing and easy to absorb resulted. They might have created hyperlinks between passages to related items of their choice, further enhancing the reader experience. They might have inserted clip art or photos they took to illustrate the passages. They might have made the content into a multimedia presentation using recording and presentation software.

That same year, I saw another demonstration of student work, a schoolwide expo of student-created books, all produced on similar laptops. Students each identified a theme that interested them, endangered species in this case, did research on the animal that they were interested in, and published their own book (using word processing software and other available digital resources) celebrating their species, explaining its survival issues, and making recommendations about how readers could help. This was transformation, with students actively engaged in science and social studies learning for a purpose and to address an audience—to make an impact in the world by being an adept learner and articulate voice. What I witnessed was middle school learning very powerfully transformed, and in the process I received insights into how teachers might use technology with their students. In using the SAMR framework, we are given a tool with which to understand the transformation of education through technology use, how to plan for it, evaluate it, and more.

USING THE TPACK FRAMEWORK

Technological Pedagogical Content Knowledge (TPACK) is a framework to understand and describe the kinds of knowledge needed by a teacher for effective pedagogical practice in a technology-enhanced learning environment.

One way we might define the digital learning environment of the future is that it will provide instruction and learning opportunities for learners that are emblematic of the best and most relevant instruction (for a given learning goal) from each of three domains:

> **CONTENT:** the body of skills and knowledge to be learned; the material to be read or viewed or reviewed or the activities engaged in (e.g., measuring, interviewing, researching, etc.)

PEDAGOGY: the body of approaches taken and efforts made to teach or otherwise foster learning of the targeted learning outcomes

TECHNOLOGY: the platform on which the learning is staged and made to happen—the tools and resources used to support the learning

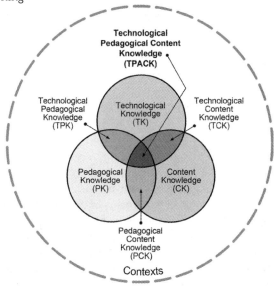

Figure 3.2. TPACK Framework. ©2012 by *tpack.org*

When these three components are skillfully and insightfully implemented, especially in a context in which the value and nature of all three and their interrelated workings are accounted for, a very rich and fruitful intersection results that represents a transformed platform for, experience of, and outcome of learning.

In a sense, preparing schools to transform what's currently done in classrooms to conform to the TPACK model, as well as to undertake all steps necessary to bring that about, is highly emblematic of the digital transformation of schools that has been anticipated.

The Teachers Teaching Teachers website presents the TPACK framework as part of a major project of the Australian Government Department of Education aimed at enabling all preservice teachers at early, middle, and senior levels to become proficient in the use of Information and Communication Technology (ICT) in education. The organization's webpage offers the following description:

In the 21st century, ICT is providing us with new ways to access and process knowledge in every field. ICT is also transforming pedagogy by providing new ways to engage learners. Expert teachers now are those who can bring together knowledge of subject matter, what is good for learning, and technology (ICT). The combination is described as Technological Pedagogical Content Knowledge (TPACK). It is more than simply adding ICT to traditional approaches. It depends upon deep knowledge of how ICT can be used to access and process subject matter (TCK) and understanding how ICT can support and enhance learning (TPK) in combination with PCK." (AUSTRALIAN GOVERNMENT DEPARTMENT OF EDUCATION, N.D.)

USING A DIGITAL TRANSFORMATION / TECHNOLOGY ADOPTION MODEL

While such documents represent some of the very best thinking from highly experienced people well versed in this sort of visioning (I was personally involved in some of Intel's early blueprint think tank sessions), they also may serve as a model of the process of understanding and planning for increasingly important technology use in schools. In this particular representation, a variety of influence factors (e.g., leadership, professional development, and curriculum and assessment) are seen against the implementation reality of the saturation of devices available to students (moving from left to right the student to device ratio moves from 20:1 to 1:1). All such "tools," though, are best seen as snapshot understandings that are representative only of best thinking and best practice at a particular moment in time. This specific approach may not fit perfectly for other schools and their particular goals and circumstances.

While the school-based digital change agent may not be able to exert influence in all the factors listed here, the model can prove very useful in brainstorming with colleagues to identify implementation and success factors and to conceive how to apply and monitor these against school technology use and learning goals. In other words, the exercise of developing a school's own technology adoption/transformation matrix is something that will help establish greater clarity about the process.

Before delving into how to bring about change, we need to understand a bit about the role of the digital change agent. This person is often, but not always, a school- or district-based technologist focused on supporting educators at the school level in the use of technology. The next chapter will characterize the digital change agent and explore their crucial role in bringing about transformation.

CHAPTER 4

The Digital Change Agent

"A leader's role is to raise people's aspirations for what they can become and to release their energies so they will try to get there."—DAVID GERGEN

Who will be the change agents that support and help guide communities of educators on their journey to shifting to a digital platform for getting their core business done? And how will those change agents function within the organizations they are part of? What sorts of roles will they adopt to get this crucial work done?

GUIDING TRANSFORMATION

It isn't difficult to see that all schools will need to have at least one person on staff who can guide the school community. Virtually everything will rely on technology: from administrative functions, like informing parents of standardized test dates and maintaining student attendance records; to essential organizational functions, like analyzing student performance and preference data and assigning them in appropriate ability groupings to classes; to the core teaching functions of distributing content materials, assigning activities through which to learn and demonstrate learning, and assessing what's been learned and making worthwhile predictions about future teaching and learning.

Approaches and resources to accomplish these tasks, which have always been central to the purpose and mission of a school, are appearing in digital form in increasing numbers and at accelerating rates. Further, these new digital resources are often easy to see as more functional and impactful than traditional predecessors; more cost effective, too. In the impending digital shift, these resources will be increasingly adopted and more traditional, paper-driven methods and approaches will be phased out.

It behooves schools to have a staff available to guide them through this shift. Successful transformation requires an intimate understanding of the school and its culture, as well as the curriculum and prevailing instructional philosophies. Even in the event that funds were to materialize for schools to outsource such guidance, it's much more likely that guidance by stakeholders who are part of the organization will prove most effective.

Consequently, members of the school's teaching staff, along with school-based instructional supervisors and some school administrators, are most likely to assume the role of digital change agent. Certainly, district-based staff members assigned to support schools may provide much-needed assistance for them. Still, "in-house" staff members will have the most relevant knowledge base to bring to bear. That is, provided that this knowledge is balanced with sufficient grounding in "next step" technology and its school-based application. It is a wise principal who is currently thinking about who on the teaching staff might step into this role. Likewise, it is a wise district-level administrator who is currently planning how to support schools in grooming and developing these individuals.

MANY HATS

Many schools already have teachers on staff who teach technology. Some are computer or lab teachers. Other schools may have media center teachers. These teachers perform important functions but may not have the knowledge and insight to take on a newer and broader role that involves being a leader of colleagues, a researcher and advisor to administrators or school leadership teams, and, to a degree, a visionary, evangelist, and advocate. The digital change agent will likely need to wear many hats.

Further, the change agent will need to understand the process of change, particularly to a digital platform. There is a broad kaleidoscope of policy, funding, philosophy, and societal climate that continues to shift as each school engages with this change. The change agent must understand and stay aware of these developments.

10 Roles of the School (or District) Digital Change Agent

1. EVANGELIST: While there is an edtech revolution going on all around the profession of teaching, teachers are busy and many are set in their ways. There are still many who fail to see the relevance, importance, and potential of technology to positively impact teaching and learning. Winning over the interest of those who aren't already engaged is important to bring about the change that's needed.

2. ADVOCATE: Moving from a traditional, paper-driven platform to one that is digital involves making changes to procedures, policies, and methods that were created to support the old and often impede the new. For instance, purchasing rules that were adopted to ensure efficient acquisition of hard-copy textbooks may not translate to pay for access to cloud-based content. The new resources may require advocacy for changes to procedures that facilitate technology adoption.

(continued on next page)

3. GREAT EXPLAINER: Technology represents many shifts. Because it is new, many see it as simply "more" to do. In reality, it makes things more doable, more practical, and easier. New ideas and profound and radical changes that technology represents will have to be explained to members of the school in order to help them see the potential.

4. MYTH BUSTER: Many myths have grown up around the adoption of technology in schools. For example, one myth is that the adoption of technology is intended to replace teachers. Myths have to be explained away in order for those unfamiliar with technology to understand and embrace it.

5. COACH: Coaching, an approach to developing and supporting professionals as they grow, is an effective method that has grown in popularity in school and district communities over the past several decades. It is proving to be an important way to ensure that school staffs cope with the digital shift skillfully and successfully.

6. PRAISE SINGER: It is often highly advantageous for change agents to share and praise examples of school community members who take risks, attempt out-of-the-box activities with students, and have noteworthy successes. Such sharing acknowledges these individuals, encourages others, and disseminates ideas and information.

7. VISION QUESTER: Beyond simply adopting it for the sake of being current, technology has the power to vastly change the goals of education as well as the methods for how they are achieved. To avoid aimless wandering and ensure success, a vision (a clear understanding of what the school is trying to do with technology and why it is attempting this) is needed. While a school community is easily capable of understanding its vision after it has been formulated, the process of recognizing that it needs one, and working on it, is not something most staff members are familiar with. So important is the vision process to successful and meaningful change that Chapter 5 is entirely devoted to it.

8. GRAND ORGANIZER: The school's technology use program likely will involve marshalling the energies and cooperation of many disparate members of the school community. It may involve cross-curricular events like technology fairs and STEM/STEAM expos; the establishment of special programs for students, like student tech support teams or extracurricular activities like student robotics teams;

advocacy measures, like fundraisers and outreach to local politicians for increased funding; and on and on. The digital change agent will have to organize and coordinate the efforts of many.

9. **LEADER:** In numerous ways, the school's technology use program must deal with outside agencies. These may be the district technology office, school and district curriculum and instruction directors, vendors and providers of resources, funders, and parent groups. The school administration will need to entrust a sufficiently aware and informed individual to both represent the school and bring back pertinent information. Traditionally, many districts have taken the SPOC (single point of contact) approach, whereby each school is required to appoint a representative to interact with the district-level technology office. The digital change agent playing this role will need to expand on this approach in a variety of ways, including fostering a vision for a complex program and communicating on behalf of that program with a variety of entities, including the district technology group.

10. **CHANGE AGENT:** This essential role requires an understanding of far more than technology. This player will need to know technology, including that which has been proven practical in the day-to-day functioning of schools. They will also need to be knowledgeable about teaching and learning, as well as the many organizational facets of a school.

SCHOOL LEADERS AND THE DIGITAL TRANSITION

In the article "8 Ways School Leaders Can Support the Digital Transition," Laura Devaney, managing editor at eSchool News, discusses how school leaders are supporting progress as schools make the shift to digital learning. She states that "administrators at the local, district, and state levels are essential to leading and supporting the digital transition in schools across the nation (Devaney, 2014)." However, an examination of the ways that these administrators can best support this crucial transition reveals that establishing appropriate and effective leadership at the school level is a favored approach. There is nothing in these recommendations to support the notion that only formally trained, formally appointed, and formally titled individuals should be leaders; actually, the opposite is often true.

The eight ways recommended in the article are:

1. Don't rely only on external programs to prepare school leaders. The leaders truly needed are the ones who are "home grown."

2. Develop and support growth at all levels. Less emphasis on formally trained administrators, more on developing leaders as they emerge.

3. Make a shift to coaching. The leaders needed can be coached by others already successful at leadership to ensure their success.

4. Create initiatives and outreach for rural district leadership development. Regardless of population density, reach leaders where they may not traditionally be thought to come from.

5. Put a premium on high engagement. High teacher engagement is an indicator of successful technology integration leadership.

6. Identify and cultivate future leaders. Those in positions of leadership should identify those with potential to lead development.

7. Authorize leadership at all points in the district. Leaders come from all parts of the district, including support and custodial staff.

8. Acknowledge leadership. The pride people develop when recognized for their incipient leadership is powerful. (Devaney, 2014)

THE COACH AS CHANGE AGENT

In her Edutopia article, "How Instructional Coaches Can Help Transform Schools," Elena Aguilar, a transformational leadership coach from Oakland, California, states:

> *Traditionally, instructional coaches have played a rather narrow role in schools, usually working primarily one-on-one with another teacher. This work is important and coaches can be instrumental in developing the skills of teachers. But, if the conditions are right, coaches can work in several additional ways to support the transformation of a site. . . . Coaches can bring teams together in healthy ways, they can support teachers to increase their emotional resiliency, and they can facilitate systems change.* **(AGUILAR, 2012)**

Of particular interest is the article's section on how coaching can be seen as a powerful method for systems change. From their vantage point, coaches can see the big picture within schools, "the way in which people are working, the impact they're having, the needs of students, teachers and administrators," and, from this position, "if they have the skills, coaches can help others see these big pictures and work towards systemic changes" (Aguilar, 2012).

TEACHER LEADERS

Many, if not most, school technology leaders will hold a teaching license, teaching position, or will have moved on from a teaching position to assume a support position or leadership role. This is as it should be. The radical change from a traditional, paper-based culture to one now altered and expanded by the shift to digital technology requires that those who would guide be well versed in the intricacies of teaching and be sufficiently accomplished in technology skills. Further, actualizing the potential of these two bodies of understanding to impact others requires a third set of skills: leadership skills. This is all the more true because those who would lead a school staff often will do so without the authority behind them of an officially designated position.

In his article, "What Do Teachers Bring to Leadership?" Gordon A. Donaldson, Jr., Professor of Education at the University of Maine, points out that "teacher leaders do not necessarily fit the leader-as-hero stereotype. Instead, they offer unique assets that come from the power of relationships" (Donaldson, 2007).

Administrators and formal and informal teacher leaders all contribute to the leadership mix. They hold the power to improve student learning in the hands they extend to one another.

In her MiddleWeb article, "7 Valuable Roles for STEM Teacher Leaders," Anne Jolly, a former middle grades science teacher and Alabama Teacher of the Year, gives some highly informed perspective on the value of teacher leaders to the expanding and increasingly important area of STEM education:

In the STEM education arena, teacher leaders are particularly crucial... every school and district needs to invest time and resources into developing STEM Teacher Leaders... to take on additional roles and responsibilities.... These teacher leaders often have more credibility with their peers than educators who are no longer in the classroom.... They're extremely useful; maybe even indispensable. **(JOLLY, 2016)**

Jolly ponders what functions STEM Teacher Leaders (STLs) would perform, what roles and responsibilities they might fulfill, and offers "a few ideas to chew on," including that STLs can:

- be involved in policy and advocacy;

- help in STEM planning & decision-making;

- facilitate professional learning for colleagues;

- find funding for programs & equipment;

- help all students receive a first-rate STEM education;

- keep STEM programs on the front burner; and

- model continuous professional learning. (Jolly, 2016)

In their Educational Leadership article, "Ten Roles for Teacher Leaders," Cindy Harrison, an independent consultant with Instructional Improvement Group, and Joellen Killion, Deputy Executive Director, National Staff Development Council, discuss the roles that teachers can play in school leadership, stating that "because teachers can lead in a variety of ways, many teachers can serve as leaders among their peers" (Harrison & Killion, n.d.).

The following ten roles are a sampling of the many ways teachers can contribute to their schools' success:

RESOURCE PROVIDER: Help colleagues by sharing instructional resources.

INSTRUCTIONAL SPECIALIST: Help colleagues implement effective teaching strategies.

CURRICULUM SPECIALIST: Lead teachers to agree on standards, follow the adopted curriculum, use common pacing charts, and develop shared assessments.

CLASSROOM SUPPORTER: Work inside classrooms to help teachers implement new ideas, often by demonstrating a lesson, co-teaching, or observing and giving feedback.

LEARNING FACILITATOR: Facilitate professional learning opportunities among staff members.

MENTOR: Mentor novice teachers.

SCHOOL LEADER: Share the vision of the school.

DATA COACH: Lead conversations that engage their peers in analyzing and using this information to strengthen instruction.

CATALYST FOR CHANGE: Serve as visionaries who are "never content with the status quo but rather always looking for a better way."

LEARNER: Model continual improvement, demonstrate lifelong learning, and use what they learn to help all students achieve. (Harrison & Killion, n.d.)

GROWING INTO THE ROLE AND OFFERING SUPPORT

Digital change agents, no matter what path they take to the role or how far along they are in the process of embracing their new role, can benefit from the following steps:

1. In a collegial manner, make colleagues aware of your intention to support an expanded, more comprehensive technology use program in the school. Seek and establish support from the school administration. Provide a rationale that stresses the need for such an initiative.

2. Engage administration and supervisors in conversations about their understandings and goals in relation to the expanding role of technology in all aspects of school business.

- Ask if they already have someone on staff they see as the tech point person. If not, express interest in supporting colleagues this way.

- If there is already someone seen as the point person, have a friendly, collegial conversation and offer to provide support for colleagues that isn't already provided.

3. Take a measure of the school community. Which colleagues are well on their way to accomplished technology use for the betterment of their students? This may be begun with a voluntary survey or by personal inquiry or observation.

4. Plan how to provide information for colleagues, wherever they may be on the continuum of adopting, adapting, and using technology.

5. Establish channels of communication for an expanded technology use program, such as a website and blog.

6. Educate yourself on educational technology and maintain as high a level of knowledge and awareness as possible. Subscribe to news aggregation services like SMART Brief on EdTech, EdWeek Digital Directions, and ISTE publications. These services can be set to deposit periodic updates in your email. Perusing and skimming this stream of information will, over time, heighten awareness of trends and developments in the field without requiring much time dedicated to reading full articles or books. For more resources and recommended outlets, see Chapter 8.

Change Agent Profile: JESSIE BOYCE

Jessie Boyce has been teaching for nine years and is a middle school math teacher at the Center for Innovation and Digital Learning at Tyrone Middle School in St. Petersburg, Florida.

In 2015, my school decided to start a magnet program within their traditional middle school. The plan was to begin with one grade level and to add one per year with the anticipation and hope that the full school would be one-to-one within five years. I was fortunate enough to be on the team from the ground up, working alongside administration to help that vision come to fruition.

The Center for Innovation and Digital Learning's mission statement is to provide "an intellectually challenging environment that encourages students to become critical and reflective thinkers in preparation for success in college, careers and citizenship in the 21st century global environment."

The initial plan was to focus on the small—88 students in a magnet program that had technology embedded in every class—but with the foresight of eventually seeing it spread throughout campus. As the team learned and implemented different things into our classrooms, we would share with others in professional development sessions or by having our peers visit our classrooms. This was two-fold: to showcase what we were doing, but also to prepare for school-wide implementation.

The original barriers began with too much excitement without fully understanding the direction we were moving in. Our team went to the ISTE conference in 2015 to gain some insight on innovation in the classroom and ways that technology can best be utilized. I was overwhelmed with excitement, realizing that there was a world of education much deeper than what I had been taught. I also realized that digital learning by no means implies simply sticking a computer in front of students and calling it a day. I learned that there is a never-ending stream of information in the education world, especially involving ways to use technology in the classroom. An important discovery was the resource of Twitter for use in the education realm. There is a constant connection to those educators who have been there, those in the trenches with you, and those with brilliant ideas to learn from. It has been a huge part of improving my educational practice.

The integration of Microsoft Office 365 has completely changed the way I run my classroom, but also the way that I look at education. Our county made the decision to purchase Office 365 for all employees in the district and our magnet piloted the students having access to Office 365 accounts, which has since gone district-wide for all students. I have realized that students can greatly benefit from having access to Office in a cloud-based manner. The use of 365, most specifically, OneNote, has allowed students to develop a greater sense of agency, taking responsibility for their work and having the freedom to move at their own pace. OneNote is a virtual notebook, with tabs and pages to organize information. Each student has a notebook for each individual class, where everything they need is located. They have one space for all assignments, quizzes, homework pages, and reflections. The days of crumpled up pages forgotten in the bottom of a backpack are finally behind us. I quickly fell in love and couldn't keep quiet about it. I have wanted to know all that I could about Microsoft, about technology in the classroom, about personalized learning and ways to bring innovation to my school. I am one who will quickly delve into books, trainings, any resource that I can to learn about my practice.

Others on campus have noticed the different things that are occurring in my classroom and some have taken the initiative to ask if they can come witness it. Administration has asked my colleagues and I (the magnet team) to provide trainings to the rest of the teachers on our campus about what is working and ways that we can move forward. I have been doing district-wide training biannually to help others bring technology use into the classroom.

While some have welcomed these trainings with open arms, others have been quite resistant. It's hard for me to put my finger on the reason for the resistance. Stereotypically, in the teacher community there is a mindset of "well this is how I have always done it and why would I change now." For obvious reasons, this is a terrible way to think because the world around us is ever-changing, including the children that we teach. Another big issue that I see plaguing the education community is the amount of work and expectations that are continually piled on. I believe that many view integrating technology into the classroom as "one more thing" that must be done.

The last thing that many want is to go to *more* professional development. But what about when that professional development is not the same old thing, but can make a drastic impact on the classroom? I think there is a huge need for professional development that is truly beneficial to teachers. PD that focuses on the areas where there is a deep need and/or deep interest, not just because some high up thought that it would be a good thing to focus on. I believe that if this were the case, perhaps many teachers that do not want to attend another training, would be more apt to partake. After all, didn't many of us become teachers because of our love for learning at one point or another?

I truly believe in providing a PD that I would want to attend. If it seems that it is going to be a waste of time, I'm not going to do it. I think that the most important part of professional development is having people walk away feeling like their time was valued and that they have learned something.

It has been my goal to make people feel comfortable with thinking a little outside of the box. I have approached this in a manner of I am not here to change what you are comfortable with, but rather to push thinking in a direction that maybe there could be some things that could be adapted to our constantly changing students and their need to be fed.

My challenge has been reaching those who feel that they have nothing to learn from me or those who feel they could not possibly make these changes because of one reason or another. I am often met with "well that is your school... my school runs differently and that would never work..." My charge for them is to find a way. That's what change is all about. Making a way out of no way.

A current barrier is the actual use of technology. While more teachers are opening up to the ideas of teaching in different ways, there is a concern with computers just becoming a replacement for a paper worksheet. The Substitution Augmentation Modification Redefinition (SAMR) model developed by Dr. Ruben Puentedura explains that at the substitution level where teachers are merely replacing the work that was already being done, just now on a computer does not have much functional value. "No functional change in teaching and learning. There may well be times when this the appropriate level of work as there is no real gain to be had from computer technology. One needs to decide computer use based on any other possible benefits. This area tends to be teacher centric where the instructor is guiding all aspects of a lesson." *(http://bit.ly/1mweDWV)*. Technology should be a platform in which we are able to reach new innovative heights, rather than staying where we have always been. A discussion needs to be had on ways that technology can be integrated in the classroom in order to change what has been done in the past, leading students to be critical and creative thinkers.

I believe that in the wake of something completely new (digital integration), it is almost a natural thought process to simply put what would already be happening in the paper-based classroom onto the computer; for example, using an ebook to replace the textbook and calling the classroom a digital one. My colleagues and I try to show the different ways that technology is being integrated. Modeling these ways allows you to see that there is so much more to it than a digital worksheet.

For those who are willing to take a leadership role to move colleagues along in this process, my advice is to not give up! Be willing to look to others outside of your comfort zone for support and most importantly, stay enthusiastic. At the end of the day, enthusiasm is always contagious.

CHAPTER 5

The Vision

"*So often, people are working hard at the wrong thing. Working on the right thing is probably more important than working hard.*"
—CATERINA FAKE, CO-FOUNDER OF FLICKR

The previous chapters addressed the need to know the new landscape of teaching and learning, the full territory. What follows is the need for each community of educators—whether it be a district, school, department, or other segment—to craft a vision of its own place within that territory. What will its home there be, how will it function, and above all, how will that community create that particular home, one that reflects the ways that technology's capabilities and possibilities help it realize the overarching goals for its students? That particular place and the community's map or blueprint for it, as well as the directions to arrive at or establish it, is its vision.

THE BIG PICTURE

An ancient Indian parable relates the story of a group of blind men who come across an elephant. Each man attempts to identify and understand the animal by touching the part closest to him. The blind man who touches the elephant's trunk believes it is a hose. The one at the other end grasps the tail and believes it is a snake. The man who strokes the tusks is sure it is a spear. The man who pats the elephant's side concludes it is a wall. And the one who embraces a leg thinks it is a tree. The elephant, of course, is much more than these perceptions, all of which are based on good sense, but which are very incorrect because the blind men are not capable of perceiving the totality: the big picture.

This situation is similar to the understanding of edtech in our schools. By now, just about every educator has heard or read about it, and many have experienced it, but only from the small niche subset of the vast total body of resources, approaches, practices, and understandings that is their particular experience. Very few educators have had the opportunity or reason to wrap their minds around the totality of the intersection of technology and education. Consequently, school staff members often have very disparate understandings of what edtech is and can be.

As the field of education approaches the impending state of digital ubiquity, the most advantageous condition for success and avoidance of counterproductive efforts will involve clarity through common understanding. While it is unlikely that all educators will ever take a full-blown graduate-level course that immerses them in an accurate, big picture understanding of edtech, assuming that there are good courses that teach this in the first place, it is important to understand this situation and need and to strategize to cope and succeed.

SUCCESSFUL TECHNOLOGY PROGRAMS BEGIN WITH A VISION

Schools are often required to produce a technology vision statement as part of a larger technology plan. This can stem from funding, accreditation, and compliance requirements imposed by a variety of entities. Certainly the school will need to satisfy these requirements, and often the principal or other administrator will appoint a point person to take charge of creating the vision statement. When the effort is handled thoughtfully and responsibly, a committee of concerned stakeholders will be convened as well. In some areas, this chain of command may be prescribed, although often the school must determine its own way to move ahead.

While the fact that it is often a formal, standardized requirement that leads those tasked to produce it to view it as a chore, the generation of a technology vision statement can also be seen as a powerful opportunity, one that can be an important step in a school's forward movement toward masterful technology use.

It's wise to focus on the important distinction between the general, overall technology vision statement and the technology *use* statement. The technology vision statement, one that historically has been the only one required in schools and districts, can cover everything from plans for hardware purchases and roll-outs of equipment to ISP and Wi-Fi expansion and distribution, budgeting to individual schools (in the case of a district plan) or intra-school departments for discretionary purchases of resources best made on the local level.

The technology use plan has emerged more recently and can be fit in as a subset of the generalized item. In fact, it would be wise to make technology use the central hub of all visioning and planning around technology in schools and districts. After all, shouldn't the way technology is to be used for schools' core business, teaching and learning, be the driver and informer for all other decisions?

In creating plans and visions it is wise, as one of the initial steps, to investigate the existence of other plans and ensure that the plan being created and its vision is consistent with and doesn't contradict or conflict with them.

ASK, WHERE IS THE SCHOOL GOING? HOW WILL IT GET THERE?

Schools that move into establishing or furthering a fully comprehensive technology use program without a vision and a vision statement do so with the very high risk of getting their program very wrong. School technology use programs are not likely to succeed without planning and accounting for a great many success factors.

Equipping a school with devices and infrastructure should be determined by how the equipment and devices will be used and not the other way around. Unfortunately, and this was thankfully much more the case in earlier days of edtech, schools often acquired things, often using up most if not all of the budget and only afterward considered, "Okay, we have this stuff, now what can we do with it?" The answer to that crucial question, far too often, was a description of activities that did little to support or improve what the school had been doing in a paper-driven hard-copy environment. Little wonder that in so many corners of education, technology has taken so long to be viewed as of value.

Resources for Creating Vision Statements ...

A Definitive Guide for Developing a Technology Vision Statement for Your School *(http://bit.ly/2BmGq8f)*. In this blog post, Kim Cofino, a teacher in international schools, outlines the process she and other members of her school's committee employed to create a vision statement for the use of technology.

Developing Technology Vision Statements by Bill Ferriter *(http://bit.ly/2AgOGeg)*

8 Guiding Questions for Conversations About Becoming a School of the Future *(http://bit.ly/2jxCKtd)*

PURPOSE AND FUNCTION

The vision and vision statement capture and communicate what the members of the school community understand and believe about education and how they understand technology can support and improve it. Best practices for edtech should dovetail with generalized understandings of instructional best practices. Goals for the use of technology should mesh with goals for education and the learning experience the school offers its students. The vision statement should reflect school culture, aspirations, and group understanding about how they are to be reached.

The statement will be an enduring (although, hopefully, periodically revisited and updated) record in the school and will serve as a touchstone to be reviewed and reflected upon when the process of coming to consensus from square one repeatedly would be terribly impractical.

Community members can turn to the statement when needed to remind themselves of what's been agreed upon and explained for those carrying out school business and planning next steps.

Elements of the Vision Statement

The vision statement defines and explains the school community's technology use, including how it applies to and addresses the following:

- Community

- Treating and supporting students and their parents

- Aspiration for students

- Teaching and learning

The vision statement includes *why* the school is focused on using technology, *how* the school sees technology as part of what it does and offers students, parents, and others (for example, particular or special themes or missions, what the school sees as its core business, how technology can help the school better achieve and address its core, general vision), and *who* should use technology and why they should.

The vision statement answers the questions: what will the use of technology accomplish for the school, and what will the school accomplish with technology?

The vision may also include:

- A statement about where the school is currently (with the use of technology) and where it wants to go in the future (in developing its technology use)

- A list of shared core beliefs concerning education, instruction, and technology

- A list of goals and behaviors that would evidence having reached them (for example, students will use technology to support their efforts to take charge of their own learning and exploration)

- A brief description of who was involved in the creation of the vision statement as well as a description of the process involved in creating it

CREATING THE VISION AND VISION STATEMENT

As the vision and vision statement is intended to express the community's understandings, it must be created as an outgrowth of community member collaboration—either through efforts to draw the input of all community members or of representatives of constituent segments of that community (including teachers, subject area departments, instructional supervisors, and parents).

The process to engage and guide the school community in agreeing on statements of its goals and values and ideas about how to achieve them may involve informational sessions to give background so that community members weigh in once they are informed.

The process is a highly specialized form of community building. It is not only a path to producing a statement that embodies a set of beliefs and aspirations, but also an opportunity to convene the community in ways that are unique and powerfully unifying.

In his blog post titled "Developing Technology Vision Statements," teacher and edublogger Will Ferriter opens up a discussion about school technology visions and vision statements by writing an open letter to principals to whom he directs some wonderfully relevant and well-framed, probing questions.

"Dear Principals," he begins. "If I asked you to explain the rationale behind the technology choices that your school is making, could you do it?"

Could you:

- Describe the kinds of things you'd like to see students doing with technology—and more importantly, how those actions and behaviors will ensure that your students and your school are more successful than they currently are?

- Describe the core technology expectations you have for every teacher and team in your building—not just those who are drawn to new digital spaces and behaviors already?

- Guarantee that every teacher in your building was aware of—and invested in—the same core technology expectations that you've embraced?

- Prove that the choices made when spending your technology budget are supporting your school's mission? (FERRITER, N.D.)

The author is asking these questions precisely to drive home the point that in far too many schools the principal would not be able to answer them adequately and that inability is part and parcel of an important, common situation, one that is holding our school communities back from fully and meaningfully participating in the digital transformation that is ready to explode at this point in the evolution of education.

Considerations for Creating Vision Statements

Why formulate a vision and express it in a vision statement?
It is often highly useful, even revelatory, to define and clearly state what a school holds as its beliefs. By focusing on and then examining an externalized statement, the community achieves clarity.

What should the vision statement be composed of?
Introductory and framing language. A few simple statements that reveal the core beliefs concerning teaching and learning and technology's role in education. These statements should be broad, but not so generalized that they are meaningless. For example: "We hold that technology can produce better learning," or "Students should learn with technology to prepare them for their future." Rather, the vision statement should allude to outcomes that are identifiable and/or measurable. For example: "We hold that appropriately used technology will provide our students with highly personalized instruction that addresses their specific learning needs as defined by formative assessment methods used in the course of instruction across the school curriculum," or "Because students will continue in technical school or higher education that will require the extensive and sophisticated use of technology, our school will make

(continued on next page)

technology use part of its instructional goals and program in ways calculated to ensure their success."

What about noninstructional technology uses?
All resources and functions within the school support effective teaching and learning, whether they are specifically directed at instruction or not. Stating this may increase the usefulness of the vision statement.

What is the process for creating a vision statement?
A successful process may be led by a staff member who is informed about technology's potential to keep the core business of the school (teaching and learning) relevant and effective. Involve the community and its stakeholders, either directly with total participation (through surveys, general meetings, etc.) or through representatives on a work committee. Include informational sessions for the community so that they are aware of the state of instructional technology, its potential, and common practices in implementation before they decide on how the school should embrace it. Ensure transparency with a high profile so that all members of the community are practically kept informed and involved. Employ a writing process that includes participants brainstorming a list of the school's beliefs about education, and then review the list with an eye toward relevance to technology (or a similar approach).

Should the vision statement be updated?
The vision statement should be periodically updated to stay current and relevant to ongoing changes in educational philosophy and practice and in technology.

 ACTIVITY

FORMULATING A VISION STATEMENT

To better understand the process of formulating a vision statement, reflect on the following questions:

- Who would you include in the planning of the vision statement and the overall technology use plan?

- How would you engage them?

- What technologies might you use to work with them and to develop the plan?

- What sorts of processes and activities would you use to engage the stakeholders/contributors to the plan document? Possibilities include surveys, large group discussions, small focus group discussions, interviews, suggestion box, and group writing efforts.

Change Agent Profile: JULIANNE B. ROSS-KLEINMANN

Julianne B. Ross-Kleinmann is an educator and a life-long learner. She has seven years of experience as an administrator, 20 years of experience as a teacher, and five years of experience as an adjunct professor. In all her experiences, she continues to hone her skills as a staff developer by presenting for national and international audiences in the areas of STEM, literacy, standards, and testing. Her passion is instructional technology in the service of teaching and learning.

"I hate technology!" I remember those words so clearly echoing around the class the first time I walked into Mrs. X's room. I was still standing in the doorway as she uttered those words, loud and clear and not only in front of me and another adult in the room, but also in front of her entire class. All those young, impressionable first- and second-grade minds sitting on the rug waiting for instruction turned their big eyes up toward me, the new technology teacher. "Yeah," shouted some, now agreeing with their teacher. I felt powerless, defeated, and angry, just like the teacher who was saying the words. I knew my goal was to turn her around. But how was I going to do that? After my encounter with Mrs. X, as I started walking across campus to my room I wondered, did everyone at the school share this sentiment and, if they did, what caused them to feel this way?

This was my first experience teaching in an independent school. And, the more I think about it I realize it, it was a first of many things all at once: first time working in an independent school; living in a new state; new home, new curriculum path. Budget cuts forced me back into the interview pool and I was hired at School X because of, first, a change to the school's schedule; second, my knowledge of teaching entry-level robotics; and, third, my ability to help create a STEM curriculum from the ground up. As the lower school technology coordinator, I was assigned to work with students in grades one through four. My initial role was prep coverage more than tech integrator but that was something I planned to change. Noticing that the tech lab was not conducive to teach STEM activities, I reached out to the middle school science co-chair for help. We worked together to co-teach one STEM lesson for my third grade classes which turned into a wonderful four-year collaborative, co-teaching, co-learning partnership model. So why did I feel comfortable to ask the science co-chair for help? Well, when the school schedule changed and an additional prep was added for third grade, I learned during my interview it was the science co-chair who researched current trends and advocated for bringing STEM experiences to the lower school.

In my search for employment, I was the one who did not do my research. I later learned after being hired, School X was more of a traditional school and not place a place where technology was a priority. As a matter of fact, School X was slowing changing their view of no screen time for elementary aged students.

Technology at School X consisted of most teachers having a Smartboard a computer and printer in their room. There was a lower school lab with desktop computers and an upper school lab with some desktops and laptops. Teachers were encouraged to use their Smartboards but minimal training was available. Most software used was accessible free online or installed on the desktops. And most teachers didn't hate technology they were detached from it, because they never had a consistent successful relationship with authentically integrating technology at School X due to high turnover in the technology department. Above all it is essential for any teacher to have support when change is involved. However, sometimes you need to reach to outside networks like ISTE to provide support and continued growth and that is one thing I did to keep abreast of the essential skills my students and teachers would need to be successful technology change agents. At School X I tried my best to help TEACH technology: build trust, create equity, advocate on their behalf, and collaborate, all while being humble and infusing humor.

It took me time to build trust with my colleague and students.But now, Mrs. X sings a different tune when I walk into her classroom. Now she says, "Hey can I borrow more OSMO's for our back-to-school night, so I can share with families how we are using technology in class?"Or, "Can you remind me the password for Vimeo so I can show Mrs. Y how to embed videos onto her blog?" My major breakthrough happened when I helped Mrs. X use technology so her students could publish their stories. After working together and successfully accomplishing this, she asked me to print a copy of their anthology for each student. I froze. This was not what I understood to be our outcome. But little did I know she had been publishing books for years with her classes and to her this was obvious. I told her I might not be able to do that. After reflection and fear of disappointing her, I did a work around, asked our new Director of Technology for funding, and created hardcover Apple Books for her class and for the school library. When I returned to her class and said I was sorry I misunderstood the end goal and offered her what I thought might be an acceptable alternative, she was more than elated. What I learned was changing the technology culture had nothing to do with technology; it had to do with really listening to the teacher and being flexible enough to prove that you listened—then they feel comfortable to start listening to you.

Here are some of the ways I helped TEACH technology at School X.

- **T = BUILD TRUST.** I responded to help desk tickets within 24 to 48 hours. Even if I couldn't resolve the issue, I made sure I acknowledged the person's request for help. I made myself visible—arriving early, attending various meetings, and volunteering around campus. I co-taught and modeled for teachers entry level applications that students could continue on their own or with minimal assistance.

- **E = CREATE EQUITY.** I shared resources and my time among students and staff. I applied for grants to bring in hardware and software. I ran after-school classes for students and workshops for teachers.

- **A = ADVOCATE ON THEIR BEHALF.** I helped to add to Mrs. X's voice. She hated technology because the technology she had wasn't working and the Wi-Fi in her building was insufficient. I was an advocate for students who wanted to run after-school programs to teach coding to their peers. I learned about Minecraft so I could help speak up for students who wanted to use Minecraft in school.

- **C = COLLABORATE WITH THEM.** I co-authored lessons, co-taught, modeled, and sometimes was an extra hand in the classroom, even when the subject was not related to technology. I made sure I listened to teacher needs first, before moving forward with plans. I arrived early, cleaned-up afterwards, and asked how could I help again.

- **H = BE HUMBLE AND INFUSE HUMOR.** I let teachers know I don't have ALL the answers and that there are times when technology does not work for me—specifically, the time I called IT support to help fix the printer that was unplugged.

Through TEACH, I was able to help teachers receive updated hardware, strong Wi-Fi, research-based apps for education, a Scratch Day event, increased authentic use of technology integrated across subjects, and, most importantly, a wonderful new mindset where they ask themselves, a colleague, or me, "what technology can enhance this lesson?"

CHAPTER 6

From Vision to Reality

"Vision without action is a daydream. Action with without vision is a nightmare."—JAPANESE PROVERB

Once a school has an understanding of what it wants to achieve with technology, something made clear and concrete through the vision process, it can more confidently address how to do so. Whatever next steps the school needs to take, the following considerations can give it a greater likelihood of success.

A major success factor is buy-in and ownership of the school's technology program and model of use. Toward that end, and to tap into the experience and accumulated wisdom and expertise of the community, as many members of the school community as possible should be included. To achieve that:

- Share the vision (this may also be seen as a facet of advocacy).

- Announce to the community that the school will be entering into the planning/ technology program development process.

- Invite input as far and early as is practical.

- Include the input of all; if not directly, then through representation in the vision itself, as well as in the planning that follows.

- Report planning progress and stages to the community. Keeping the process open and transparent and making efforts to keep all stakeholders informed about progress will provide momentum and support.

Following are some recommended methods and approaches to move from vision to reality. What's particularly important here is not only the to do items mentioned, but that they are presented in a sequence that places each item in an order that makes the most contribution to the whole, end-to-end process. Rather than simply following this list, it is probably best that you and your collaborators comprise your own list of implementation and success factors and then lay out a plan to reach a significant, reasonable goal for each.

ASSESSMENT

It would be practically impossible to find a school in which technology isn't used to some degree for teaching and learning, as well as for the myriad administrative chores needed to support them. As we've seen already, it's important to know what's possible in terms of school technology use—asking what's the state of the field and what would it look like when a school in an ideal scenario without limitations and constraints supports its program optimally with technology. On the other hand, it's even more necessary to understand where one's school is on a continuum that holds that ideal scenario as a goal to be achieved down the road, to understand where the school is at the moment with the ideal functioning as a background for understanding.

With an understanding of the learning environment a school aspires to establish, the first step toward achieving it is to ascertain its current state of technology capacity and use. Then, planning can be done in an informed manner that is calculated to change what's current to an understood future.

Some of the more important implementation factors to ascertain include the following:

- What resources are available, in what quantities, and to whom? This may include hardware, infrastructure (everything from power connections, connectivity, and bandwidth). Most schools already have a technology inventory, something that may be required by districts or state departments of education. Where is the technology kept, who has access to it, is it being used and how? These further questions are harder to find answers for.

- What level of expertise is evidenced by the overall body of community members (in terms of handling the technology and, especially, applying it to student activities, learning goals, and teaching practices)?

- What tech-supported practices and approaches are currently in use in the school?

For each of these factors, determine what needs exist for further and better implementation. There are resources available for this, or you could simply use generic tools like online surveys, shared documents, and easy-to-create tables.

A simple self-assessment questionnaire distributed to each teacher (easy to accomplish online using a tool like Survey Monkey), requiring ten minutes or less to answer, would be a good way to begin this process. Ask what technology is available for each teacher to use, how often, and how it is used (what sorts of activities are students engaged in through the use of the technology).

This will give a quick snapshot of how the staff uses technology. You might include questions about what additional activities would the teacher begin to use technology for if they were made available. The simple act of responding to such a questionnaire will serve to engage teachers further in technology planning and awareness. A comparison of the survey with the inventory will quickly reveal gaps and inconsistencies. It may be the case that there are more resources available than the teaching staff is aware of.

NEXT STEP PLANNING AND GOAL SETTING

Planning meaningful next steps for the school can be a complex process. Targeting the acquisition of equipment and resources is not an appropriate next step item on its own. Past efforts have seen schools focus on resources over practices, which often led to school staffs, both technology specialists and core curriculum teachers, having to put their heads together to figure out what could be done with resources already acquired, as opposed to which resources to acquire because they are needed to support targeted best instructional practices. Similarly, PD alone and out of the context of holistic planning won't make much difference.

One approach that promises transformational progress would be to have the community focus on a shift to technology-supported practices that involve a body of simple devices that have wide application in teaching and learning—laptops, Chromebooks, or tablets, for example, paired with interactive whiteboards. A learning management system (LMS) is another resource that can do a great deal toward bringing an entire school staff into the ranks of technology-using educators. Keeping to a small group of highly flexible resources will keep maintenance and PD requirements minimal.

On the practices and activities side, identify a body of new practice for each teacher following the SAMR model. Include some new practices that involve simple *substitution* of what's currently done in the teacher's classroom through traditional, hard-copy content with a digital version (for example, students move from consuming print content to digital on a simple short story). Include *augmentation* of such practices (for example, students move from consuming the same piece of content to selecting their own story based on person interest). Include *modification* of such practices (for example, students, in addition to reading the story of a chosen author, research and access audio clips of the author reading and reciting the story). Include *redefinition* of such practices (for example, students produce a slideshow or video as a book trailer to be uploaded to the web as advertising to convince other students to read the story.)

Each teacher, with the partnership and approval of an instructional supervisor, can propose a body of such new (to their practice) activities, vetted as standards-based or otherwise core to required curriculum and instruction. The school instructional technologist may also provide links to video tutorials or webinars to ensure that new skills the teacher will need are explained over a period of time, with success building on success and further goals being set. Such a model may produce a transformative effect on the staff's knowledge and skill sets and tech use commitment and repertoire of practice.

CURRICULUM PLANNING

Whatever the instructional approach, whether it simply be "implementing a textbook" or challenging students to undertake sophisticated learning projects that will have them researching, learning, and producing a product to demonstrate what they've learned, there are digital corollaries that offer expanded possibilities over traditional text-based, instruction.

Conceive of technology integration as the ongoing process of planning and implementing curriculum that makes use of the advantages of technology, not as after-the-fact shoehorning of technology into student activities.

An approach to planning instruction that reflects a good awareness of the place for technology would place learning outcomes as the prime planning factor, with instructional practices in support of those, along with supporting digital resources. This would hold true not just for that small portion of the overall body of learning incomes that specifically have to do with technology itself, but for all outcomes across the curriculum for which tech-based teaching and learning advantages can be identified and for which resources to support them are available.

PROFESSIONAL DEVELOPMENT AND SUPPORT

There is much attention on, and activity around, professional development (PD) for educational technology use. However, unless it is tied to well-thought-out, focused goals and plans, it amounts to little more than activity for its own sake, even if it appears to be something needed or wanted at the moment.

PD is not an answer to the question, "What might possibly move our school community's technology program forward?" Rather, it is an essential element of an overall initiative that represents value when it fits properly within the greater whole. In my own career, I've seen far too much PD given that had no concrete plan for teachers to implement the skills they learned. Unless a skill set or series of instructional methods and techniques that is taught in PD is connected to an actual plan or opportunity for the teachers to use them, unless they have the instructional need, the time, and the resources required, then PD will be a nicety, but not something that is likely to produce any results.

Again, following the approach of identifying activities and practices supported and enabled by technology and placing them first, as the organizing priority for planning, professional development will likely need to be arranged for teachers who need to handle the technology itself, as well as learn how to apply it in the context of the teaching and learning practices it is intended for.

Delivering PD

The first era of edtech saw the vast majority of PD for its implementation delivered through infrequent workshops, an approach that produced poor results in precipitating the change in schools from traditional, paper-driven modes of teaching and learning to digitally supported learning. There are now numerous modalities that can be employed, constituting a body of approaches that can account for the challenges of time and scheduling, funding, and workflow. The result is that an informed school can arrange for the PD it needs in ways that are practical and that will produce the hoped-for effect.

Much has been written about providing professional development to further technology use in schools. Here are some crucial bottom-line points:

1. Even when there is access to PD content that is just right, teachers generally are too busy teaching and preparing to take advantage of it, at least through the traditional workshop approach. Consider alternatives like video tutorials and recorded webinars, so that teachers can get important PD material when they have some spare time or when they want to multitask (for example, by listening to PD podcasts while driving to work).

2. When planning other aspects of a comprehensive technology use program, like resource acquisition and curriculum development, consider what average teachers will need to learn, how much they will have to learn, and how they will learn it, before committing to next steps.

3. Develop a matrix that plots key skills and bodies of knowledge as part of PD planning with the understanding that not all teachers will be able to get all the PD they want or need. Most will be able to receive just a small part of what they might need in any given school year, and the PD they do receive had better be relevant and effective because of that. Assume that far less PD will be able to be delivered than would be ideal and plan around that.

PD Delivery Methods: It's NOT Just Workshops!

Professional development and "workshop" are often assumed to be one and the same. There are, however, other ways of delivering PD. In addition to workshops, some well-established approaches include the following:

WEBINARS: Live, virtual sessions in which presenters share ideas, illustrations, and demonstrations online using digital conference resources that allow for voice, image, document, media, and screensharing and that facilitate communications between participants through audio, group work management resources, chat, and other features. Webinars are generally delivered live, but often recorded so that their content can be reviewed at a later date.

PODCASTS: Radio show-like recorded audio presentations as well as VLOGs, which use video as well as audio for the same purpose and distribution scheme.

COACHING: An ongoing situation in which a mentor and mentee confer and collaborate on improving the mentee's knowledge, skills, and experience base in a process of gradual and continuing improvement.

EMBEDDED PD: A "teacher trainer" visits a classroom and gives a demonstration lesson, engaging the students in authentic, technology-supported learning—the class's teacher, and perhaps others, observes and participates alongside the trainer.

TUTORIALS: How-to demonstrations in the form of text, video, audio, etc., that illustrate how to use and apply technology in the context of instruction.

PROFESSIONAL LEARNING NETWORKS (PLNS): Groups of professionals with similar interests and goals who share information and expertise, generally informally, and often online.

Why different methods? Often one method is more appropriate and effective than others, and selecting the proper method is a key success factor. For example, online tutorials can be accessed on demand when a teacher needs to know something specific, "just in time." Or perhaps the teacher's schedule is too tight at certain times; listening to a recording of a webinar when there is time may be the solution. A podcast can be replayed, and the listener can go to just the right spot in the audio recording to relisten to things of importance or interest. There may also be cost factors that render one method more advantageous than others.

Planning for Successful PD

An activity I assign to my students involves the creation of a graphic like the one below. I require them to submit a table like this with at least five rows filled in. A planning tool like this, while simple, is likely to greatly support a PD program.

Table 6.1. PD Planning Tool

PD NEED	RECIPIENT	DELIVERY METHOD	EVALUATION METHOD(S)	NEXT STEPS
What skills and bodies of knowledge are important to be learned and will make a difference because devices, digital resources, and curriculum to use them will be in place?	Which colleagues really need to learn this and are likely to use what they learn to improve their teaching practice and student learning experience?	There are many ways to impart technology use information and skills; which one is the best for this particular need and/ or will help conserve precious and scarce resources and capabilities as it is learned?	How will you know that the learning was the right learning? That it was delivered effectively? That it was used by the PD participants? That it made a difference?	What's needed to arrange for this PD offering to be taken? Are there barriers?

Establishment of a Support Program

Simple issues that crop up inevitably can short-circuit even well-thought-out programs. Proactively preparing for these eventualities is its own success factor, a potentially crucial one. After PD has been delivered, teachers may need a few reminders about simple tasks: how to launch a resource on a device, which option to choose in order to save work, how to run an online maintenance check, who to turn to for repairs or pointers. These tasks don't need full-blown PD or one-on -one service; often they can be handled by providing simple support, partners to turn to for information or insights that escape on at the moment, or knowledge of where to go to get additional ideas or services.

The following approaches can be used to establish a support environment that will keep a technology use enrichment and expansion effort moving forward and successful: blogs, discussion boards, PLNs, peer learning partners, student tech support teams, websites prepared in anticipation of this need to present FAQs, and more.

SCHOOL TECHNOLOGY ADVOCACY

Advocacy for school technology is one of the important items that an instructional technology specialist may need to address in the role of leader. Over time, it is likely that he or she will need to explain and defend technology or key aspects of it. Further, in order to keep decision makers focused on the importance of maintaining the program and expanding it, he or she may have to engage in advocacy efforts.

The need for advocacy for technology stems from several sources. First, many programs within a school must vie for attention and support. Many, such as the arts, athletics, chess, and career education, may be perceived as nonessential and risk being cut or simply not receiving the support they require. Schools have a natural tendency to shift priorities and, as some things are afforded higher status or focus at the moment, the natural tendency for decision makers seems to be to cut others. It's shortsighted, but a common situation.

Second, many educators simply don't get the importance of technology. They are aware that there is a buzz about technology in the field of education, even requirements for its use. Still, they don't personally see the value and the excitement. Teaching is a difficult, time-consuming job, and taking on something new and unfamiliar represents a massive amount of uncertainty and what appears to be extra work. It is not uncommon for technology enthusiasts and advocates to expend attention and effort simply in sharing with other school staff members their understanding of technology's worth, purpose, and potential in hopes that they will see it the same way and enable technology to assume its rightful place in the school.

This lack of understanding can extend, at times, to students as well. Yes, even digital native students may not see the connection between technology—something they are fond of in the context of entertainment, gaming, and phone use—and learning. Certainly, there are parents who don't fully understand precisely what technology offers. They may believe that students should learn technology because the world of work will be dominated by it, but don't understand or approve of other applications of it.

The key to effective advocacy is simply to explain the advantages and potential that technology has for teaching and learning and to help those trying to understand this see the difficulties likely to be encountered along the way in accurate proportion. Understanding the common considerations of those who are hesitant or negative about technology and being prepared to offer easy-to-understand and acceptable alternate points of view is what is required.

Edtech advocacy on the local level may involve fund-raising and grant writing. Or it may involve gaining the attention of colleagues, perhaps by lobbying for school administrators to give it some limelight by placing it on school staff meeting agendas or including it as an option for professional development days. It likely will involve organizing a school technology fair or including a technology expo as part of a parent evening.

Local-level educational technology advocacy may involve inviting local politicians or community leaders to share the school's experience with technology, which may pay off down the road in needed support or funding.

Myth Busting as Advocacy

One of the school technology change agent's most important roles is that of explainer, a job that includes dispelling myths and replacing them with clarity about technology's use and value.

Perhaps the greatest myth about instructional technology is that it is a solution to a problem. Seen from that unrealistic and uninformed vantage point, it is to be expected that it would disappoint. Technology is the solution only to the problem of there not being technology. In reality, schools should use technology because technology is the resource and practice set that people in all fields (education being one of the few holdout stragglers) favor to get their business done. When technology is used in banking or research or medicine or law, for example, it is not considered to be a miracle solution to that field's overarching problems. It is used simply because it is a highly effective way to communicate, to store and retrieve information, to analyze and process, and on and on. It is only logical that schools should follow.

Advocacy Resources

While it may be difficult to have impact on the local level, by engaging in efforts led and supported by organizations such as ISTE, one can help make a significant impact.

ISTE Advocacy Network *(iste.org/advocacy)*

ISTE Advocacy Toolkit *(iste.org/advocacy/advocacy-toolkit)*

ISTE directory of state affiliate organizations *(iste.org/membership/affiliate-directory)*

ALLIANCES

Don't overlook alliances through memberships and participation. Various organizations—some of them requiring a fee, but many free—provide the opportunity for school affiliations and offer various types of support. For example, schools involved with student robotics may want to participate in FIRST LEGO League, which hosts robotics meets and competitions for students and whose websites provide robotics programming tutorials and tips and content materials. One important aspect of such affiliations is that, once schools become involved, they are members of an active community of teachers and students who share and benefit from the knowledge and experience of one another.

There are many such programs that schools can affiliate with, including the following:

- The KidWind Challenge: "The ultimate wind turbine design competition."

- Destination Imagination Team Challenges: "Our Challenges are open-ended and enable students to learn and experience the creative process while fostering their creativity, curiosity and courage."

- iEARN Distance Student Collaboration Program: "Learn with the world, not just about it."

Large technology resource providers are another source of affiliation that may provide services and guidance, content and resources, peer partnerships, and community. Microsoft, Google, and other technology companies offer much to schools who affiliate themselves. They offer school technology leaders opportunities for support in planning and offering staff members resources and training.

CONTINUOUS SCHOOL IMPROVEMENT (CSI)

CSI is a model that can be used to guide and inform the transformation of traditional schools into digital learning environments. This is a goal that doesn't conform to the standard model of targeting goals with the expectation that they will be achieved, fully and measurably, and then moving on to another goal. The process is ongoing; one can better understand it as a continuous improvement cycle.

In an article on the School Superintendents Association blog entitled "Never Good Enough: Tips for Continuous School Improvement," Mark A. Smylie, author of the book *Continuous School Improvement*, shares the following:

The Process of CSI

CSI is driven by a strategic cyclical change process. Many versions of this process can be found in the education literature. Most contain the following steps:

1. Clarify your school's mission, vision and core values.

2. Determine where your school is with respect to its vision and values, using evidence to identify differences and assess likely reasons for those differences.

3. Set goals and objectives for addressing those differences.

4. Identify strategies to achieve these goals and objectives and develop plans for implementing them (including developing necessary human and material resources).

5. Implement these strategies.

6. Assess their implementation and outcomes, feed information back into the first and second steps, and begin the process again.

Several factors increase the likelihood that this basic process will be effective.

- Readiness of people and the school organization to support the process.

- Centrality of student learning to the school's mission, vision and core values and to the continuous improvement process.

- Primacy of high quality, relevant and useful data.

- Inclusiveness of the process, meaning involving everyone at one time or another and focusing on every aspect of the school.

- Integration of the process into the core functions of the school. (SMYLIE, 2017)

ACHIEVING THE GOAL

In his article entitled "Leading and Learning for a Successful Digital Transformation," Steve Webb, superintendent of Vancouver Public Schools, states, "Education, like so many other aspects of our society, has been undergoing a digital transformation. Accepting this reality is inevitable. Embracing it would be wise. But my district has chosen to go a step beyond that as we strive to lead the transformation" (Webb, 2014). He explains that digital transformation in his district involved a process that engaged hundreds of staff and community members in shaping its future.

Webb's story is a fascinating overview of a process that included reflection on what's really important in having the district not just acquire and deploy technology but embrace the changes in educational thinking and practice that go hand in hand with the informed use of technology for education.

Change Agent Profile: WHITNEY WADECKI AND ROBYN MCKENNEY

Whitney Wadecki is a first grade classroom teacher and Robyn McKenney is the District Technology Coach for grades K-5 at Waterford School District in Waterford Township, Michigan. This team has worked to develop a library of classroom-proven activities that are successful to the specific culture and needs of a small district.

Whitney grew into a technology leadership position after working and planning closely with Robyn on many projects and activities. They quickly realized the power of collaboration in providing excellent instruction for their students. Another significant impact was that peer teachers were much more likely to embrace activities designed and implemented by other classroom teachers.

Often, activities and ideas spread by word of mouth or when people see them posted in the hallway or at an event. When one teacher finds meaning or success with an activity, he or she shares that success with other teachers in the building. Those teachers speak to Robyn about implementing the activity in the computer lab, or speak to Whitney about implementing the activity in the classroom. Whitney and Robyn maintain an ongoing dialogue, making suggestions or recommendations on how that activity could be integrated into other curricula or classrooms.

The collaboration with Whitney and Robyn has been especially powerful in moving ideas forward because Whitney has "classroom teacher cred" with the whole staff and understands classroom dynamics and realities that impact technology use. She is innovative and willing to take risks with technology. She models this for all teachers and her classroom provides a snapshot of a culture that facilitates tech use. Whitney is always willing to share resources, lessons, or materials. Whitney's classroom often provides an environment for implementing new ideas, but the pair's collaboration extends past Whitney's grade and many of their ideas are broad. Conversations and collaborations with Whitney inform the work that Robyn does across the district. This is an example of how one or two people's ideas can be shared with many others. Often times, in the sharing process, they are built upon or improved.

Robyn works in three schools and shares projects from one teacher or school with teachers across the district. She co-teaches in with classroom teachers in the computer lab and develops (and models) lessons for computer lab paraprofessionals to deliver when she is not present. This is a powerful way to deliver PD, model tech use, and help teachers to gain access and comfort with technology. When Robyn develops lesson plans or resources for lab instruction or tech integration projects, she shares them with any teachers who wish to pursue them. Additionally, she creates many lessons in response to teacher requests or discussions with grade level teams (examples of things that have come up are internet scavenger hunts and virtual museum visits) and often works with teams to develop specific activities or projects. She then shares them across a grade level.

One example of building success comes from the implementation of Google Apps for Education (GAFE) in first through fifth grade. Most teachers were inexperienced and therefore very nervous about the transition to GAFE and whether any benefits would outweigh the obstacles they perceived. Administrative support for professional development in one school provided the support needed to develop a cadre of "champion" teachers. In working with this small group of teachers, we were able to amplify their confidence and enthusiasm to bring other teachers on board. Whitney's students were able to demonstrate competency logging in and using Google MyMaps, thus setting a benchmark and establishing credibility. In parallel, Robyn developed diverse lab activities in GAFE that allowed teachers to learn alongside their students and gain experience. These activities are interwoven through curricular contexts. This approach alleviates discomfort and hesitancy from teachers and builds confidence and competence.

Robyn and Whitney have explored numerous apps and worked together to determine which are "high leverage" and lead to the higher levels of learning. Coding has been a significant area of growth and they have moved from simple activities on *code.org* to more diverse applications such as Scratch, robots, and drones. They collaborate continuously and brainstorm ways these apps can be used across the grade levels.

The team's guiding principle is that the use of technology should be purposeful, empower learners, and lead to higher levels of learning. This has given them greater credibility as they introduce new technologies because teachers trust that their learning goals are meaningful.

There is always a concern that technology is being used as entertainment or that we are substituting "flash" for substance. In every activity, Robyn and Whitney consider the question: Will the use of this technology move us toward transformational learning on the SAMR continuum, or are we merely substituting? Their goal is to augment or transform and they share that goal explicitly with teachers. One example is using the app Shadow Puppet Edu (*get-puppet.co*) to create a book review rather than having the students publish using word processing. At first, teachers were somewhat hesitant to embrace this strategy. Then they saw the amount of problem solving, technical expertise, collaboration, and communication skills involved in this approach.

Hour of Code was introduced to Whitney's and Robyn's school in Fall 2014. The school was awarded with a $10,000 grant that was used to purchase iPads. This was the first technology purchase beyond computers. Robyn and Whitney worked together to integrate iPads into Whitney's first grade curriculum. Their successes encouraged others to take risks with the iPads. The principal was very supportive and dedicated Professional Learning Community (PLC) time to teaching and guiding teachers through different apps for the iPads. Excitement and a community of sharing propelled usage of iPads throughout the school. In less than three years, the iPads are in constant use.

Whitney frequently assists teachers in planning or makes suggestions of projects or activities they might try. She offers formal and informal PD. Robyn works with all elementary teachers in the three elementary schools and co-teaches in the lab with more than a third of the elementary staff. She develops plans for the remaining classes by reaching out to teachers to see what they are working on in class, and then finding technology lessons to fit their needs. She also offers PD and resource development.

Through our experiences with *code.org*, we realized that coding provided significant opportunities for students to problem solve, fail productively, and iterate. We showed teachers how to get their feet wet with coding and emphasized that the goal was not just to write code, but to engage in higher levels of thinking and learning. Many teachers embraced coding, but others were hesitant because they felt they lacked expertise and might not be able to adequately support their students. This was an excellent opportunity to engage in a discussion about letting students be leaders of their own learning.

Because their students were absolutely loving coding, Robyn and Whitney knew they could do more. In Fall 2017, they kept asking themselves, what's next for coding. After attending a few conferences, Robyn and Whitney decided to purchase their own robots to see how we could use them to extend coding. After experimenting with the robots, Robyn and Whitney introduced them to their students to experiment or, what we like to call "plearn," play learn. The students fell in love with the robots. Robyn and Whitney then developed two concurrent days devoted to robots. On "Robot Days," every student kindergarten through fifth grade and every classroom teacher attended. Every class attended for an hour and experienced two 25-minute "stations." Robyn and Whitney introduced some different robots and gave the teachers an opportunity to see how engagement with robots facilitates higher levels of learning. One was exploration and challenges using Ozobots. The students were able to explore, solve puzzles, and collaborate to find ways to use the Ozobots. The other station was a STEAM activity in which kids were given a robot and iPad, a challenge card, and some legos, construction paper, tape, and scissors. Kids had to build the character delineated on their challenge card using the supplies available, then program the robot to exhibit that character's behaviors. Success was measured by whether people could guess the character. Teachers and students loved it so much that the overwhelming feedback was: When are we doing this again? Can we do this in our classroom?

This was so successful and highly valued that teachers requested additional experiences which led to "Innovation Station" days where kids engaged in many coding and robot experiences.

The students that were not high flyers in the classroom often emerged as the robot experts. They found an area where they could shine. All of the teachers in the building were introduced to robots and were able to see the grit and perseverance it took for the kids to be able to program them. Now, the students and teachers ask for the robots by name. We have also expanded our coding program into an afterschool club. The initial success at Quaker Hill led the way for all three elementary schools. The PTA at every school heard about all the great things Whitney and Robyn were doing and has supported them by purchasing robots each school.

Through this experience Robyn and Whitney have discovered that their partnership has more power to transform learning and impact numerous learning environments than either person could achieve through their individual efforts.

CHAPTER 7

Change and Resistance

> "Change is hard because people overestimate the value
> of what they have and underestimate the value of what
> they may gain by giving that up."
> —JAMES BELASCO AND RALPH STAYER

I f the change agent is going to play a key role in
bringing about a profound, needed change,
his or her understanding of that change is
essential. Also helpful is a sympathetic view
of the resistance to change—especially to the
integration of education technologies—and
knowledge of methods for addressing or
overcoming this resistance.

WHAT'S CHANGED AND IS CHANGING?

On the simplest level, what's changing in our schools is that technology has appeared, keeps turning up with greater frequency, and draws more serious attention to itself. It is essential to understand why this is so, in order that proper choices can be made and maximum positive impact derived. After all, the purpose of adopting technology is not as an end unto itself. Understanding the reasons behind it, so that the community's general goals are in sync with it, is an overarching success factor.

Digital Transformation, a Crucial Next Step?

What's looming for all schools everywhere goes beyond the simple adoption and integration of technology. Digital resources and the practices they will be used to support are in many cases transformative; students and teachers are enabled by technology to do things better and to do better things. In other words, the use of technologies will change what a school's goals are, how it operates and accomplishes these goals, and the degree of success it will have.

Digital transformation then, is the state of schools changing themselves to better accomplish their goals; some that they have always had and some that have arisen as the possibility to do better things has emerged in the light of technology, the great enabler.

While the progress of this dramatic change in education is happening at a faster pace than many of the major changes that have come before, it is still unfolding in stages. We have experienced the development and emergence of digital technologies, the slow experimentation with them, their gradual adoption and adaption to the business of school, and their general acceptance in schools and in popular use. The next phase, one in which the majority of things done in school will be handled through the use and support of technology, much as it is for the greater society beyond school, is just beginning. This phase we can call the digital transformation of education.

DIGITIZED TRADITIONAL LEARNING VS. DIGITALLY TRANSFORMED LEARNING

The adoption of technology in the context of transforming education involves much more than simply adding technology to a model of teaching and learning that was developed in a pre-technology era. This is a key understanding for all those who wish to bring instruction better in line with current educational theory and philosophy, many elements of which, like social learning, the need for personalized learning, and the pursuit of higher-order thinking skills, are not well served in the traditionally organized, paper-driven classroom but are now made possible and easily implementable in the emerging digital learning environment.

Teachers who understand teaching and learning in terms of the traditional model, that is, the one that evolved to serve the pre-digital age way of working and learning, often fail to see the advantages of technology and its applications.

Further, when they do feel the need to make technology a feature of what goes on in their classroom, they often attempt to force new resources and practices to conform to old models. In the process of doing this they may defeat the advantages technology offers.

For example, in the pre-technology, traditional model of school, great stress was put on the acquisition of memorized facts, which in turn were considered legitimate and significant evidence of being "educated." A classic example of this would be the practice of having students memorize the capital cities of the 50 states.

In the technology-transformed world in which we currently live, such learning accomplishments have paled. Virtually everyone has access to a connected device throughout the day and, while some may be able to recall from memory that the capitol of North Dakota is in fact Bismarck and not Fargo, now anyone can reach for their device and search the correct answer in a matter of seconds. Ironically, there are still schools in which this sort of learning is part of the instructional program. More surprising, there are numerous digital resources that will "drill" students to support them in these memorization tasks, and there are schools that acquire these resources and use them as part of their technology use program.

Once learners are freed to a degree from chores like memorizing state capitols, they can be engaged in thinking-oriented activities, like comparing Detroit, the capitol of Michigan to Guangzhou, the capitol of Guangdong, China—both manufacturing centers—to determine the factors that may account for the failing economy of one and the expanding and prospering economy of the other.

When palm-sized digital calculators first became available to all, there was much debate about allowing students to use them in math class. At the time, it was accepted as gospel that memorizing math facts was an unquestionable, highly valuable goal of math class. It was common to hear critics back then demand, "What are those kids going to do when they're not near a calculator? How will they function?" Currently, though, it is virtually impossible to find oneself in a place where there are no calculators; they are built into almost all the devices that vie for our attention in a world crowded with technology. And we know, too, that allowing students to use calculators empowers and enables them to tackle greater goals than the memorization of facts and basic skills.

In both examples, we can see how the emergence of a digital resource has transformed learning, both in its goals and its methods, and has enabled students to engage in deeper varieties of learning that are more relevant for the world in which they live and will take their place. And we can also see that the possibility exists for schools to ignore these changes, to attempt to continue on in the technology era as they did before, and even attempt to counterproductively put transformational digital resources at the service of goals and practices that have faded in importance because of the very emergence of digital technologies. While these are simple examples, the phenomenon underpinning them brings up deep and far-reaching questions.

Not all the technology-driven changes in our curriculum and its teaching are so clear-cut and easy to comprehend. At times, schools and the educators who work in them may simply overlook what's special about the transformative power of technology on teaching and learning. For example, teachers may have students use word processing resources to prepare their final version of an essay—that's applying technology to a traditional task but not making much of a change beyond a neater physical appearance. Compare this to copying and pasting the text of the essay into a browser and uploading it to a class blog, where it will be published in the true sense of the word by making it available to an audience who may read it and provide feedback in the form of comments. A proven and highly favored framework for the teaching of writing holds that this part of the cyclical process (publishing and eliciting feedback from an audience) is a highly valuable dimension of the learning process, one that makes an important difference to the learner. It is important to note that this part of the cycle, although a long-sought element, was virtually impossible to provide to students before technology in the classroom. A blog makes it possible for students to move from the status of content consumers struggling to imitate real writers to fully becoming content creators and published writers.

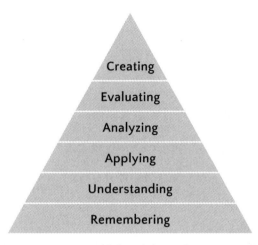

Figure 7.1. Common representation of Bloom's (revised) Taxonomy of intellectual behaviors associated with learning.

There are many ways that technology changes learning and how it is fostered and achieved. Educators often focus on Bloom's Taxonomy (shown in Figure 7.1) as a way to conceive, understand, and plan learning activities. Looking at a common hierarchical representation of the taxonomy and its six constituent intellectual behaviors, we can see that technology may be used to engage students in activities that address all of them, while noting that in the pre-technology era stress was placed on the lower-end behaviors, remembering and understanding, which were behaviors for which pre-technology activities were possible and practical. With the advent and adoption of technology, a far greater variety of more elaborate activities are now practical to implement, thus transforming teaching and learning

Is it the technology that's changed the way educators now conceive of what's important to teach and learn, or is it that philosophical changes have driven a quest for resources that could make alternate learning goals and teaching practices practical?

There is some truth to both perspectives. Approaches like project-based learning, student research, authentic learning experiences (student publishing), collaborative student learning (in small groups), and others that educators now accept as defining practices relevant in today's instruction were around long before technology was available in our classrooms. However, they were difficult for most teachers to implement, and the advent and adoption of common classroom technology has changed that. They are now doable by all teachers who understand their value and who want to take them on. And this perspective is an essential element of moving schools further into meaningful technology use of the kind we may call digital transformation of education.

SHIFTING PARADIGMS

Technology is an essential partner to a very serious shift in the educational philosophy. This new paradigm has emerged in the era of digital technology, differing greatly from the old one that was developed to serve agrarian economy and manufacturing economies.

Some of the principal differences between the two paradigms are depicted in Table 7.1. Most importantly, technology is associated with the implementability and practicality of items in the new paradigm. This is the main takeaway that those who would support and guide colleagues in making this shift need to point out and explain. The shift from one paradigm to another is always difficult, and it is the understanding of the new one and its promises that moves people from one to the next.

TABLE 7.1. Differences Between Traditional and New and Emerging Paradigms of Teaching and Learning

OLD (TRADITIONAL) PARADIGM OF TEACHING AND LEARNING	NEW AND EMERGING PARADIGM OF TEACHING AND LEARNING
Teacher-centered instruction	Student-centered
Memorization (and skills listed at the lower end of Bloom's Taxonomy) as the sole body of types of learning addressed by instruction	Addressing all, including those listed higher in Bloom's Taxonomy
Knowledge transfer as a model for teaching and learning	Discovery learning, constructivism, social learning, authentic learning
Average student as target	Each student is unique with personalized (and differentiated) learning as an instructional ideal
Learning about things	Learning by doing actual things (authentic, real-world activities)

A shift can also be seen in the learning environment and how the adoption of technology has changed it. Table 7.2 compares the traditional classroom and the emerging digital learning environment

TABLE 7.2. Differences Between Traditional Classrooms and Digital Learning Environments

TRADITIONAL CLASSROOM	EMERGING DIGITAL LEARNING ENVIRONMENT
Classic, text-centric content items (textbooks)	Digital, media-based content (audio, video, animated, VR/AR) that addresses students' accessibility needs, can be annotated by teacher, etc.
Content is exclusively created by the publisher	Content may be created or modified by the teacher, or even created by the student
Content is static	Content is interactive
Materials are one-size-fits-all	Materials are adaptive to student need and interest
Targeted at average student (middle of class)	Materials and activities are individualized
Supports study (learning about things)	Supports active learning by doing, exploring, experimenting, discovering (hands-on activities such as robotics)
Classroom is self-contained and isolated	Learning environment is connected and unrestricted by physical location (virtual field trips, collaborative and exchange "distance" projects, ask an expert/author, etc.)

Management, administration, and support tasks are also made less time- and labor-consuming, as well as more effective and efficient by the application of digital technology, freeing up teachers to focus on their core responsibility, instruction. Some of the tasks made easier by automation and digital technologies include:

- Rosters, attendance, student records

- Distribution of content and assignments

- Collecting student responses

- Ordering and inventory of materials

- Parent outreach and communication

 ACTIVITY

CREATE A "BIG PICTURE" REPRESENTATION

School digital change agents can use this sort of activity to plot the kinds of edtech resources and practices available and currently in use, with the goal of reaching a comprehensible, holistic view that the change agent may share with the community they serve. This is a valuable exercise, whether you do the activity in full or simply embrace the frame of thought it embodies.

1. Make a list of items associated with school technology and categorize some of those you feel are most important. List things that teachers do to integrate technology into their teaching. Include resources (websites, apps, software, hardware, etc.), general approaches (project-based learning, student online research, game-based learning, etc.), and specific practices (class blogging, student digital portfolios, video book trailers, etc.), and any other category of technology integration that you feel you should include.

2. Create a flowchart of how technology is used in schools and how it is integrated into the curriculum. Sort the things you include into categories. Give each category a name and a shape.

3. Organize the shapes however you feel makes the most sense and so other teachers might learn from them. You may want to prioritize them, with the more general or important items in larger shapes and placed toward the top of your diagram; or, you may want to organize them in other ways that make sense to you. You may want to repeat some things and place them in more than one spot. You may want to use arrows to connect items. You may want to play with colors, fonts, and objects to make your ideas clearer to yourself and your audience.

4. Reflect on and discuss the things you discover.

RESISTANCE TO CHANGE AND OVERCOMING IT

One of the dimensions of the edtech revolution that is important to understand is that many professionals in the field have resisted the adoption of technology.

In the very beginning of what we can call the edtech era of schooling, that period of time in which teachers began to use technology as a body of resources for teaching and learning, resistance wasn't an issue as there was little sense that all teachers should participate. There simply were a few teachers who became aware of technology that could be brought into the instructional environment and used, initially as a teaching tool, and then as a resource to be put directly into the hands of students.

In this beginning phase, teachers had to either seek approval from supervisors to use technology, or, as is often the case for pioneers and innovators, simply did what they felt was right, adopting the position that it's easier to beg forgiveness than to seek permission. Either way, these early adopters were representative of the opposite of resistance.

Fast forward more than a decade, and within the broad institution of school there emerged some pockets of progressive practice in which certain teachers, for specific purposes, were issued technology resources and expected to use them with their students. This was primarily so that the district could point to this participation as evidence that it had, indeed, begun the process of making technology part of its body of defining programs.

In the '90s, I was put in charge of Project Smart School, a special project undertaken by the New York City Board of Education to "computerize" the schools. In this project, middle school classrooms were equipped with groups of desktop computers. The emphasis was generally for math and science classes to receive the equipment. The sense was that equipping all classrooms citywide was too much of a stretch in terms of resource expenditure and change management, and that only certain subjects were an appropriate match for use of digital technology.

It's at this point that the phenomenon of teacher resistance to the use of technology appears. Even with the cautions and limitations built into the initiative, resistance by teachers was noted as one very common reaction to their being put into the participating cohort by their principals.

Since that time, the body of possibilities for use of technology as part of conducting the core business of school has expanded greatly, and the ways and conditions for which teachers are invited, expected, or mandated to use it have multiplied greatly as well.

When reflecting on the uses of school technology, we understand that while a teacher, in performing the timeless act of taking attendance, for example, may initially grumble about being expected to do so. And perhaps after many years of performing this function with paper and pen, this teacher might attempt to evade a new method that requires entering data digitally through a uniform interface the school or district has adopted for this purpose.

We understand that ultimately such resistance is futile, can't be tolerated by an administration that has standardized its own housekeeping procedures on such a method, and that, within a short period of time, even resistant members of the teaching staff will fall in line.

Furthermore, much technology is used by teachers to support teaching and learning. Within this broad category, some technology use may simply involve switching the format of a standard textbook distributed to all members of a class to a digital, screen-carried body of course content. And yes, in such a scenario, some teachers, those who have successfully conducted their classes using a hard-copy resource, may be resistant to changing and put up a good fight for as long as the paper version is still available and relatively relevant and its use tolerated by supervisors.

On the other hand, there has emerged a very large body of instructional practices, particularly that portion of teaching that involves the implementation of more progressive philosophies and approaches to teaching (for example, the use of interactive digital content items, in-class web-based research, and student publishing projects) that truly requires teachers to become involved in a varied palette of technology use. It's from this context that we see a good deal of teacher resistance. And, many would add that it is from this shift in philosophy of approach and the goals of teaching and learning that arise both the insistence from supervisors to make use of it and the resistance to do so from some teachers.

For those who take on the mission and responsibility of guiding, supporting, and encouraging groups of teachers to adopt technology and make good use of it, with the improved educational experience of their students as the underlying rationale, reflecting on and understanding teacher resistance to the use of technology can be an important factor in getting past it. Digital change agents can plan for and avoid resistance, as well as cope with it and overcome it.

In an *Education Week* article entitled "10 Reasons Your Educators Are Resisting Your Change Initiative," we are treated not only to a fine opening to considering this phenomenon, but to a wonderful switch of expectations about responsibility and approach to dealing with it. School staff who've been around for a while will recognize that the items on the list are well-known perennials that crop up in their professional experience repeatedly from time to time. The list includes the following:

SURPRISE, SURPRISE!: Items that are sprung on administrators and teachers without notice.

EXCESS UNCERTAINTY: Change without information or explanation.

LOSS OF CONTROL: Items that foster the feeling that one's practice is going in directions one can't keep up with and exert professionalism on.

LOSS OF ROUTINE: Change may bring loss of familiar routines and habits.

WE'VE SEEN THIS BEFORE: Expectation that the initiative is temporary and will stay incomplete.

LOSS OF FACE: Change implies the former way was wrong; administrators and teachers may feel embarrassed.

CONCERNS ABOUT FUTURE COMPETENCE: Educators question their ability to be effective after a change.

RIPPLE EFFECTS: Change in one area can disrupt other projects or activities.

MORE WORK: Organizational change often increases workloads.

SOMETIMES THE THREAT IS REAL: Change often creates winners and losers.

The piece concludes with sound advice: "As a school leader, if you want your change initiatives to be successful, you *must* address these issues. More important than whether *you* think you've addressed them is whether *the resisters* believe that you've addressed them. It's what is in *their* heads and hearts, not yours, that's important" (Education Week, 2011).

To that informed perspective on generic change in schools, we can add predictions about the causes and forms of resistance that are involved in promoting the greater adoption and use of technology in schools.

WHY DO TEACHERS RESIST USING TECHNOLOGY IN THEIR CLASSROOMS?

Much opinion on teacher resistance to technology adoption and use has been written and published and is freely available on the web. This body of thought and opinion is so extensive that a comprehensive review and listing of all causes for this, both those that stem from teachers and their personal beliefs and preferences and those that schools unwittingly integrate structurally into their technology programs, is beyond the scope of this chapter. However, an article by Dawn Casey-Rowe entitled "Why Do Teachers Resist Using Technology in Their Classrooms?" is representative of the thinking by school-focused technology leaders that is based on their direct experience in attempting to move groups of teachers to fully embrace technology.

The piece, which appeared as a blog post, matter-of-factly points out that teachers resist technology for a few reasons:

THEY ARE TOLD WHAT TO USE. "Any top-down command to use technology risks being a flop unless it's something teachers wanted... Let the users—teachers and students—decide, and you'll get a higher adoption rate with a much higher return on investment."

THEY GET TOO MUCH TECH. "I call it being 'tech drunk.' All of a sudden, the miracle of technology comes from the heavens to the classroom and teachers naturally want to use it all. That's also a recipe for disaster because it means teachers may be too excited to try everything without thinking of an overall goal for deploying the tech to reach the end goal."

THEY'RE WARY OF WASTING TIME. Teachers are often afraid of putting valuable time into learning and implementing new tech, only to find it's not supported, breaks, or isn't upgraded or renewed.

"IT'S AN EVALUATION YEAR; I'M NOT TAKING CHANCES ON THAT." In a climate when a bad evaluation affects a career, and student test scores matter, the result is you'd be a fool to take a chance like that— that's how people think (CASEY-ROWE, 2016).

The piece concludes with some very sage wisdom, well worth keeping in mind:

> The best way to get teachers to use tech and to continue to try new things is to allow the freedom of choice, build trust that it'll work without blocks and breakages, and to replace the high-stakes fear with high-fives for taking chances. (CASEY-ROWE, 2016)

EDTECH MYTHS AND HOW TO DEBUNK THEM

In strategizing to avoid and overcome teacher resistance to technology, a particular focus should be made on what can only be described as edtech myths. These beliefs, some of them around for a very long time, apparently have an appeal to those without direct experience, because of their seemingly good sense or truthfulness. On the contrary, they are typical of popular stories that have accompanied many of humankind's steps forward, particularly those that threaten to upend the status quo. Just as during the great age of exploration when many expressed fears of falling off the edge of the flat earth if they ventured too far from the familiar coast, at its core, edtech threatens the status quo substantially and takes people into unfamiliar waters. That people imagine great peril in this is not all that surprising.

Myths about the use of technology in teaching and learning include unrealistic claims about its power to improve and "fix" education, as well as claims that it is dangerous or negative. It should be noted that overblown claims about the positive improvements that come with the adoption of technology are destructive in their own way because, as with all things that promise to deliver improvement, eventually accurate and balanced evaluations are forthcoming.

A good rundown of some of the common myths that make digital transformation more difficult was given by Rebecca Recco in the EdSurge article, "Five Myths About Classroom Technology (And What to Do, Instead)." Importantly, these may be based on part truths; they are accompanied by passages that set the record straight, along with recommendations on how educators and digital change agents can foster a proper understanding of the ways that technology can impact the issue positively.

Myth: Technology fixes all of your or your students' problems

RECOMMENDATION: When planning a lesson, add a technological component only when technology improves the learning experience. For example, having students experience painting on an iPad doesn't give them an opportunity to really experience paint. But having them create a painting using tempera paint, and then using an iPad and a green screen to photograph themselves in their own painting, would be a really good use of technology.

Myth: Technology is dangerous, so we have to limit access to everything

RECOMMENDATION: Rather than restricting access, we should be training students in digital citizenship so that they can safely and successfully use technology at school and at home. Administrators, train teachers to properly monitor students as they work on the internet, and give teachers administrative tools and privileges so that they can more easily supervise their students' technology use. Handle student and teacher misuse by removing their access individually—not limiting responsible users' access to useful materials.

Myth: Technology leads to student success—just look at the data!

RECOMMENDATION: Students learn best and use higher-order thinking when they are creating things to share with other people. Get students involved in creative learning, and they will be using technology to learn and create rather than regurgitate and earn points. For starters, check out challengebasedlearning.org, a site where students can practice solving real-world problems "through efforts in their homes, schools and communities."

Myth: Educational gaming improves student achievement

RECOMMENDATION: Find games that allow students to create things, such as Minecraft or Pictoboldo. Better yet, find games that allow students to create games to teach others about things they learn.

Myth: Technology is less meaningful than traditional learning

RECOMMENDATION: Technology creates opportunities to move outside the classroom and into the world to experience things that students would never experience in a traditional classroom. Try taking your students on a digital field trip to Alnwick Castle, the Taj Mahal, or the Giza Plateau using Google Maps. Or, to take it a step further, have students give a "live" report using a green screen program like DoInk Green Screen (Recco, 2016).

While edtech in many ways is associated with improved teaching and learning, the technology in and of itself is not a silver bullet for fixing problems. It is an enabler, making numerous progressive education approaches and practices finally doable and practical. It is these approaches and practices that are the improvements, not the tool set that makes them possible. Technology is not a fix or a reform or a panacea. It is a resource set, a powerful one that makes good education possible and effective.

Resistance is common and can be expected, although it can be rendered a relatively harmless companion to success. Generally, it relates to fears, some of which may be based in sensible assessment of actual possibility, while some stem from unrealistic fears of the unknown. These fears can take many forms and be related through a wide range of narratives.

There are a great many more fears than those included here, and the digital change agent is likely to encounter a good number of them. It is wise to embrace them, because turning them upside down renders them powerful discussion points from which to better understand and use technology. By embracing realistic expectations and proactive planning, colleague resistance to technology will not be an insurmountable obstacle.

Change Agent Profile: NICOLE ZUMPANO

Nicole Zumpano has been a teacher in several Chicago Public Schools. She pioneered establishing social media as an important, professional, community-building body of practice.

In the summer of 2014, I was interviewing for a technology integration specialist position at a Regional Gifted Center in Chicago Public Schools. As we walked the building, I saw remnants of many of the amazing things that had happened during the school year and asked the principal why they weren't sharing this on Twitter. His response was that as a regional gifted center there was already a lengthy waiting list and therefore no need to advertise (and he didn't have a Twitter account.) I explained that it wasn't about advertising; it was about building your brand, controlling your message, and sharing the incredible work of faculty and students. I told him if I was hired starting a school Twitter feed would be one of my top priorities.

Fast forward a month later and I'm a member of Coonley Elementary's faculty. As promised, I started a Twitter feed for our school. I began by spreading the word to the teachers and developing posters for their classrooms simply stating "Coonley is now on Twitter! Follow us @CoonleyES." Chicago Public School students start the day after Labor Day so our first week only has four days. For each day, I created Twitter prompts: "What do you love about Coonley?" "What are you looking forward to this year?" "How will you contribute to your classroom?" and "Describe Coonley in three words." For those not yet on Twitter, I invited them to have their students write their answer on the board, post-it, or poster paper and take a picture of it. I then tweeted the picture for them. Doing this advertised our new account, built momentum for Twitter and excitement for the new school year. I create opportunities for the school community to share their voice via Twitter throughout the school year. For winter and spring breaks we use hashtags such as #cougarholiday and #coonleybreak to follow the adventures of our students. At the end of the school year each student creates a six-word memoir of their year. I schedule three of these a day to go out over Twitter each day in June that we are in attendance and then post the entire slide show when we are finished.

Throughout the year, I offer assistance to teachers in several ways. I encourage them to join Twitter if they haven't already. When entering classrooms, if I see something wonderful I prompt them to tweet it. I follow each teacher on my private account and make sure to like, retweet, and advocate for them with my followers. I created a list of all teacher Twitter accounts and distributed it, making a big deal to the rest of the faculty when a new person joins. I then offered suggestions on ways to use Twitter via my blog and held professional development sessions. This year, when teachers contributed to the opening week Twitter prompts I put personalized candy thank you notes in each teacher's mailbox. The key to sustaining this new initiative was to make sure it continued living, and wasn't a one-and-done opportunity.

Each year our Twitter base continues to grow (The principal now tweets!) and teachers who were new to the platform have blossomed. One example of this is a second grade teacher, Sam @CarpenterCougar. As a coach, Sam has been my greatest success story at Coonley. Not only does he regularly tweet, he has created a separate account for his students who tweet daily—in second grade! His students (@2ndCougars) talk about their day, take pictures, and craft their own posts (moderated, but not "fixed").

This is the third year we have had our Twitter account and we continue to grow each year. I advocate by creating bulletin boards featuring teacher tweets and teacher account information. I continue to write blog posts about how we use Twitter, ideas for use in general, and even how to start your own school account (*zumpanotechlab.blogspot.com*).

Although Coonley Elementary was a highly successful school prior to establishing a Twitter account, by creating one we have shared our community with the world as well as what best practices in education look like. We model positive digital citizenship for our students. Teachers who may not see each other daily now catch glimpses into their colleagues' classrooms. This has led to new collaborations and discoveries, such as, "Hey, that looks like something I would like to try." I appreciate that my administration had an open mind and took a chance on the initiative of a new employee three years ago. I'm proud to be a pioneer of this movement and look forward to continuing to share our students' and teachers' voices.

CHAPTER 8

Going for It!

"Our very survival depends on our ability to stay awake, to adjust to new ideas, to remain vigilant, and to face the challenge of change." —MARTIN LUTHER KING, JR.

This final chapter includes resources and approaches to further help find and manage opportunities for professional learning and support. The following items are offered to help the digital change agent cope with our rapidly expanding field's overabundance of possibilities. This section can be seen as a menu from which digital change agents can flesh out their personal to-do lists for powerful beginnings and next steps that will impact their organization's technology use program.

GET INFORMED, STAY INFORMED!

I often speak to my graduate students about our work, that of instructional technology/education leaders and digital change agents, as having to be done with a veritable tsunami of ideas and information continually cresting overhead, growing all the time, and threatening to drown us.

Perhaps I exaggerate, but my students and I agree that it can often feel like this. Importantly, coping with the vast and rapid stream of information and opinion is a necessary part of the job that comes with the territory. What I do personally, and what I recommend very strongly that my students do as well, is subscribe to a handful of online news and practice-oriented publications, ones that will deposit an aggregation of synopses of articles and opinion pieces in my email inbox. I find that I keep up pretty nicely by skimming through these condensed nuggets on a regular basis. I manage to spot trends and judiciously pick and choose a few items of particular interest to read in full, perhaps a dozen each week.

Below, I've listed the publications I'm most familiar with. I've not only read all of these at times, but written for a few of them as well. Actually, there are two lists: my personal favorites and others that I've read and learned from and recommend. But again, it's a tsunami we are coping with, I can't read it all.

I strongly recommend that you review these (and any others you may become aware of), pick three or more, and subscribe to them. By simply browsing through what turns up, and of course taking a few deep dives into things that seem to merit it, over time you'll experience impressive growth in the scope of what you know and in the quality of the opinions you form.

My Personal "A List"

EMPOWERED LEARNER *(iste.org/empowered-learner-magazine)* ISTE's membership magazine, available to all online.

SMART BRIEF ON ED TECH *(www.smartbrief.com/industry/education/ edtech)* "By combining technology and editorial expertise, SmartBrief delivers the most relevant industry news—curated daily from thousands of sources—in partnership with leading trade associations, professional societies, nonprofits and corporations" (SmartBrief, Inc., 2018).

EDUTOPIA: GEORGE LUCAS EDUCATIONAL FOUNDATION
(www.edutopia.org) High-quality content with very much of an (experienced) colleague to colleague feel and perspective. Solid teaching advice, often involving technology.

FREE TECH 4 TEACHERS *(www.freetech4teachers.com)* More than 58,000 daily subscribers. Established by Richard Byrne, a former high school teacher, its purpose is to share information about free resources that teachers can use in their classrooms.

COMMON SENSE MEDIA *(www.commonsensemedia.org)* Practical information (including resource reviews) presented with a family orientation, slanted toward the current media- and technology-rich environment youngsters are learning in.

GETTING SMART *(www.gettingsmart.com)* This online publication offers a broad range of articles on highly relevant topics concerning teaching and learning, often involving technology.

EDTECH DIGEST *(edtechdigest.wordpress.com)* Insightful content, including trends, videos, interviews, cool tools, and pieces on emerging resources explained, often with an insider perspective. Offers email-based subscriptions.

CREATIVE EDUCATOR *(creativeeducator.tech4learning.com)* An online magazine (and more) that offers in-depth insight into how technology tools and fully developed instructional practices can provide rich, creativity-oriented activities for students.

THE INNOVATIVE EDUCATOR *(theinnovativeeducator.blogspot.com)* This frequently updated blog offers often "out of the box" ideas to make teaching and learning vibrant, relevant, and effective.

TECH & LEARNING *(www.techlearning.com)* Blog format publication offers a rich aggregation of insightful, up-to-date thinking and reporting from a wide variety of practitioners and thinkers.

More High-Quality Content and Perspective

DITCH THAT TEXTBOOK *(ditchthattextbook.com)* This blog, by teacher, author, and speaker Matt Miller, shares inspiration for infusing technology and creativity into teaching.

EDTECH MAGAZINE *(www.edtechmagazine.com)* This magazine offers both K-12 and higher ed versions of online content across a wide variety of edtech coverage.

ESCHOOL NEWS *(www.eschoolnews.com)* Monthly print and digital newspaper addressing all aspects of edtech.

EDSURGE *(www.edsurge.com)* This useful resource "delivers insights and connects those exploring how technology can support equitable opportunities for all learners" (EdSurge, Inc., 2018).

CONVERGE (CENTER FOR DIGITAL ED) *(www.centerdigitaled.com)* Provides a wide variety of edtech-oriented content as well as research, infographics, guides, special reports, and more.

THE JOURNAL *(thejournal.com)* Reporting on education technology since 1972, *THE Journal* informs district leaders, administrators, and educators of the latest developments and trends in edtech.

Of Special Interest

EDTECH UPDATE *(www.edtechupdate.com)* Website and newsletter that bring together the best content for education technology professionals from the widest variety of industry thought leaders.

Also, I highly recommend you set up some *Google Alerts* for news on specific edtech themes of particular interest to you.

TAKE A WEBINAR

Webinars are a high-quality approach to professional development. The advantages should be apparent—webinars can be chosen and attended by those who are interested in particular topics from a very large body of offerings available. Further, a great many webinars are recorded, so while attending the live session does require one to commit to a specific time, taking advantage of recorded webinars allows for PD virtually anywhere, anytime.

The following are samples of webinars that are highly relevant for digital change agents, addressing concerns specific to that role. Focused searches online will turn up more:

EDTECH LEADERS ONLINE WEBINARS *(courses.edtechleaders.org/resources/chat)* ETLO provides free *webinars* on topics related to *online* and blended learning.

EDWEEK EDUCATIONAL TECHNOLOGY WEBINARS *(www.edweek.org/ew/webinars/education-technology-webinars.html)* Browse *Education Week*'s collection of webinars on edtech. These virtual broadcasts address the use of technology in the classroom. All webinars are accessible for a limited time after the original live streaming date**.**

SETDA (STATE EDUCATIONAL TECHNOLOGY DIRECTORS ASSOCIATION) *(www.setda.org/events/webinars/public-events)* SETDA offers events and webinars for the public. SETDA's work is not only of interest and geared to members but applies to educators, policymakers, and the public.

EDCHAT INTERACTIVE *(www.edchatinteractive.org)* These webinars replace the typical "talking head" webinar experience with awesome interactive online PD.

GET CONNECTED

Join a PLN for Edtech Leaders and Participate

Joining and participating in PLNs is empowering. Reading the opinions and experiences of colleagues is worthwhile and fascinating, as is responding to items that resonate for you and posting your own questions, queries, requests for assistance, or lessons learned that others may benefit from. Start by perusing ISTE's own body of PLNs, some specifically geared to leaders and technology coordinators.

Find or Organize an Edcamp

Edcamps are free, organic, participant-driven, unconferences that empower educators to maximize professional learning experiences and peer networks. Learn more at *edcamp.org*.

Produce a Technology Fair

Stage an event to highlight the wonderful and worthwhile things done and learned with technology in the school already, a perfect place to gather momentum for moving forward. (See the feature on technology fairs at the end of this section.)

Make a Getting Started Announcement

Start a "next steps" blog to inform, inspire, and move your school into the digital shift. Setting up a blog is easy and can be done quickly using resources such as Blogger *(blogger.com)*, which is free and fully featured.

Get a Conversation Going
Set your blog preferences to encourage colleagues to post their comments.

Pledge to make your school future-ready

The Future Ready initiative launched in November 2014 at the White House ConnectED to the Future Convening. District superintendents that sign the Future Ready District Pledge commit to foster and lead a culture of digital learning in their district and to share what they have learned with other districts. While the Future Ready program is conceived as a network of districtwide, top-down initiatives, there is much in the framework and the pledge itself that can be adapted to guide local-level efforts to move school programs further toward comprehensive, defining approaches to the use of technology. To learn more and take the pledge, visit *futureready.org/about-the-effort* and then use the Future Ready Framework to guide your program! *futureready.org/about-the-effort/framework*.

The following item appeared in the ISTE Technology Coordinators PLN Bulletin Board. It was shared by Christine Jones, Coordinator of Educational Technology for the Palmdale School District in Palmdale, California.

Producing a Technology Fair

A technology fair is a high-profile event that can strongly demonstrate the value of technology. Here are some tips for putting one together.

- Start planning now!

- Provide food. Charge at least $25 per person to cover the cost of food, or reach out to a vendor to cover the cost.

- Use *Eventbrite.com* to do ticketing, even if your tickets are free. Make everyone register through the site. Eventbrite will allow attendees to print their own tickets.

- Use *Sched.org* for creating and distributing an electronic schedule. It's not free, but they offer a low-cost plan for schools.

- Open registrations for presenters now. Plan to have one presenter for every 25 people attending. Offer presentations that will interest your audience.

- Get a keynote speaker. If you can't afford to pay for a keynote, tap into Google for Education and see if they will send a speaker, or ask someone you know who is energetic and fearless.

- Model your conference after one you have attended, such as ISTE or CUE.

- Ask vendors to pay a small fee to have a booth.

- Find a location (a school site), choose the rooms you will use, make a map, and create signs to guide people.

- Talk it up! Advertise at local school meetings, administration and superintendent meetings. Create a buzz by putting the event out on social media. Create a website. Make it easy for people to find information about the event.

- Consider allowing administrators to attend for free. It's important for them to be there with their teachers, and they might be motivated to use their school budgets to pay for their teachers to register.

- Get help! Have people do some of the work or you will be overwhelmed. Pay staff to help with extra hours, especially on the day of the event. You will need people to scan tickets for check in, help serve food, keep restrooms clean, set up, and take down.

We ran our event at a net positive last year. We have enough to pay for this year's conference. You can do it. Think big and overplan!

MOTIVATE YOUR SCHOOL COMMUNITY

By starting the conversation and raising awareness, important discussions can take place and pave the way for digital transformation. The following ideas offer inspiration into ways to reach those in your school or district who may be resistant to change or simply uninformed when it comes to technology integration.

ORGANIZE A STUDY GROUP ON HOW TECHNOLOGY TRANSFORMS EDUCATION AND SCHOOL. Offer to guide a group of interested colleagues to research how teachers in similar situations may be using technology. The group can identify articles of high relevance for the school. Thus the preparation and light reading of a digest will serve the full community and help inform the school when it is ready to take on a more formal initiative for technology use. One example that conforms to this model is EdTech Digest, which provides full articles with a short summary up front *(edtechdigest.wordpress.com)*.

ISSUE A REPORT (from the study group) on the impending digital shift and how the school may best cope with and participate in it. Taking a position often has the effect of generating interest and participation

HOST DIGITAL CHANGE PRESENTATIONS. Invite individuals outside the school to make presentations (at required meetings and PD sessions, for example). They may be providers or experts on "next level" digital change initiatives, like schoolwide adoption of an LMS or a productivity suite of applications (such as Google Classroom and/or G Suite).

SET UP A WEBSITE to share successful or exceptional technology use within the school and to share resources and expertise to encourage replication among other members of the school community.

ENLIST SUPPORT FROM THE PARENTS ASSOCIATION. Often schools have parents who are adept with technology or who have professional involvement with it. Others are eager to contribute time and effort to the school and are particularly interested in doing so in the context of programs that the school is struggling with or that represent self-identified areas of essential growth that rely on parent input and contribution.

SURVEY YOUR SCHOOL. Find out what technology is available in your school, which colleagues use it and how, which skills and practices the staff would like to adopt and receive PD for, and more. This information is important to get started. Conducting information gathering is easy and will announce and get participation for the changes to come.

CONCLUSION

After an evolution that spans more than a quarter century, it appears that educational technology has "clicked." It has moved beyond its initial status in schools as a novelty and optional special resource and practice. The speed of its evolution and expansion has increased tremendously. It is now possible to find a resource or tool or application that addresses just about every facet of school and the work and life that goes on in it. However, with so many uses and resources it is easy to focus on the trees instead of the forest and miss the overarching themes and purposes of technology in our schools.

Why is this so important? Unless an understanding of the overarching purposes and potentials of technology in schools is gained and embraced, it is impossible to bring it in line with the overarching purposes of education in general. The result has frequently been much activity around the adoption of technology, but little far-reaching change for the betterment of students, at least not when comparing what's possible with what's actually understood and done. Yes, it's good for a high school graduate to know how to operate a computer; far better though that he or she learn more expansive, relevant, and sophisticated bodies of knowledge and skills in all of the various subjects they've studied during their high school experience—in other words, the transformed brand of learning made possible in those subjects through the effective and focused use of technology in the teaching and learning of them.

It is not enough to believe that technology is commonly in use in the world beyond school and therefore take the stance that to prepare students to take their place in the world of work they must learn about technology while they are still in school. While there is truth in this, it is a much too simplistic truth. The fact is that students learn a broad range of subjects during their school experience, and each of the fields covered in those subjects now relies heavily on technology to get its work done. In our classrooms student learn about the work of writers, researchers, scientists, engineers, and mathematicians, all of whom employ technology as basic, required, and expected resources. When our students follow that example, they are not engaging in something that's "special," they are simply doing the same things that are done out in the real world that they are being prepared to join when they graduate.

References

Aguilar, E. (2012, April 5). How instructional coaches can help transform schools. Retrieved from *www.edutopia.org/blog/instructional-coaching-transforming-schools-elena-aguilar*

Australian Government Department of Education. (N.D.). What is TPACK? Retrieved from *www.ttf.edu.au/what-is-tpack/what-is-tpack.html*

Casey-Rowe, D. (2016, February 4). Why do teachers resist using technology in their classrooms? Retrieved from *www.quora.com/Why-do-teachers-resist-using-technology-in-their-classrooms*

Common Sense Media. (2017). Mission Control for the 21st Century Classroom [Review] Retrieved from *www.commonsense.org/education/app/google-classroom*

Devaney, L. (2014, September 30). 8 ways school leaders can support the digital transition. Retrieved from *www.eschoolnews.com/2014/09/30/support-digital-transition-834/*

Donaldson, G. A., Jr. (2007). What do teachers bring to leadership? *Educational Leadership, (65)*1, 26–29.

EdSurge. (2018). We are EdSurge. Retrieved from *www.edsurge.com/about*

EdSurge. (2015). Finally! Knewton Opens Adaptive Learning Platform to Teachers and Learners. Retrieved from *www.edsurge.com/news/2015-08-28-finally-knewton-opens-adaptive-learning-platform-to-teachers-and-learners*

Education Week. (2011, May 20). 10 reasons your educators are resisting your change initiative. Retrieved from *http://blogs.edweek.org/edweek/LeaderTalk/2011/05/ 10_reasons_your_ educators_are.html*

Ferriter, W. (n.d.). Developing technology vision statements. Retrieved from *http://blog.williamferriter.com/2011/01/25/does-your-school-have-technology-vision-statements/*

Harrison, C., & Killion, J. (n.d.). Ten roles for teacher leaders. Retrieved from *https://wvde.state.wv.us/schoolimprovement/principalstoolkit/documents/TenRolesforTeacherLeaders.pdf*

Intel Corporation. (n.d.). Intel's education transformation: Technology adoption model. Retrieved from *www.k12blueprint.com/sites/default/files/Intel-Education-Transformation-Technology-Adoption-Model.pdf*

Jolly, A. (2016, November 13). 7 valuable roles for STEM teacher leaders. Retrieved from *www.middleweb.com/33329/developing-teacher-leadership-for-stem/*

Microsoft Corporation. (2015). Education Transformation Framework: Best-practice guidance for successful school system change. Retrieved from *http://az370354.vo.msecnd.net/whitepapers/school-systems-planning/18206-EducationTransformationFramework-Brochure-151124.pdf*

Rebora, A. (2010). Change agent [Interview]. Retrieved from *www.edweek.org/tsb/articles/2010/10/12/01richardson.h04.html*

Recco, R. (2016, May 7). Five myths about classroom technology (and what to do, instead). Retrieved from *www.edsurge.com/news/2016-05-07-five-myths-about-classroom-technology-and-what-to-do-instead*

Remis, K. (2015). LMS enhances K12 instruction: Systems increase engagement, provide quick access to digital resources and help teachers with administrative tasks. Retrieved from *www.districtadministration.com/article/lms-enhances-instruction*

SmartBrief. (2018). Our Company. Retrieved from *www.smartbrief.com/about/our-company*

Smylie, M. (2017). Never good enough: Tips for continuous school improvement. Retrieved from *www.aasa.org/content.aspx?id=13702*

U.S. Department of Education. (2010). The Digital Transformation in Education: U.S. Secretary of Education Arne Duncan's remarks at the State Educational Technology Directors Association Education Forum. Retrieved from *www.ed.gov/news/speeches/digital-transformation-education-us-secretary-education-arne-duncans-remarks-state-edu*

Webb, S. (2014, October 9). Leading and learning for a successful digital transformation. Retrieved from *www.edutopia.org/blog/leading-learning-successful-digital-transformation-steve-webb*

Index